T3-BSJ-818

THE moon

From earliest recorded history, man has been strangely fascinated by the moon—its silvery beauty, its remoteness, the mysterious force it exerts upon the earth. It is not surprising that this majestic satellite of the earth was worshiped as a god many centuries ago, nor that now, in this more sophisticated era, the moon should be one of the chief objects of scientific study and the prime target of space exploration.

Both secular and sacred literature has much to say about the moon, and the Old Testament is replete with poetic references to this heavenly body which in Psalm 89 God calls, "My faithful witness in the sky!"

In this Heritage volume from Tyndale House Publishers, author Richard Wolff brings into focus much historical and scientific data, and illuminates this material with an examination of the place of the moon in God's Word, the Bible. The reader will be moved to exclaim in awe, with the Psalmist, "When I look up into the night skies and see the work of Your fingers—the moon and the stars You have made—I cannot understand how You can bother with mere puny man, to pay attention to him! ... And yet You have put him in charge of everything You made...."

THE
MOON

Richard Wolff

UNITY SCHOOL LIBRARY
Unity Village
Lee's Summit, Missouri 64063

 Heritage Edition

Published by
Tyndale House Publishers
Wheaton, Illinois

Coverdale House Publishers Ltd.
London and Eastbourne

Distributed in Canada by
Home Evangel Books Ltd., Toronto, Ontario

Library of Congress
Card Catalog No. 71-86226
Copyright © 1969
by Tyndale House Publishers
Wheaton, Illinois

Printed in U.S.A.

design: Kathy Lay

The moon has always exercised a strange fascination. Ancient Babylonian astrologers carefully observed the moon from the top of temple towers called ziggurats. These lofty structures in the form of a pyramid served as temples to the moon-god, and the shrine at the top was used as an observatory.

Worship of the moon figured prominently in early pagan cults. The city of Jericho was named for the ancient moon-god. Ur of the Chaldees was a city dedicated to Nanna or Sin, the moon-god. The ruins of the ancient

ziggurat still dominate the area. Built about 2100 B.C., the temple was 200 feet long, 150 feet wide and 70 feet high. It was the spectacular monument of the moon-god worshipers.

The God of glory appeared to Abraham when he lived in Ur of the Chaldees. In response to the divine call, Abraham left the city of the moon-god and moved to Haran. It was not easy to escape the influence of fanatic moon-worshipers. The city of Haran was also dedicated to the moon. Once again the divine call reached Abraham who, in obedience to God, left the city behind, not even knowing where he was to go. Pagan worship was displaced by trust in the living God. Abraham believed that God was Lord of the moon.

A formal command against the worship of the earth's satellite was issued:

> *Beware lest you lift up your eyes to heaven, and when you see the sun and the moon and the stars, all the host of heaven, you be drawn away and worship them and serve them . . .*

Job denied that he had ever saluted the moon as it sailed in beauty across the sky.

The temptation was not always successfully resisted by the chosen nation. But those who had placed their trust in God echoed the joyful assurance of the Psalmist:

I will lift up my eyes to the hills.
From whence does my help come?
My help comes from the Lord,
*   who made heaven and earth.*

He will not let your foot be moved,
*   he who keeps you will not slumber.*
Behold, he who keeps Israel
*   will neither slumber nor sleep.*

The Lord is your keeper;
*   the Lord is your shade*
*   on your right hand.*
The sun shall not smite you by day,
*   nor the moon by night.*

The Lord will keep you from all evil;
*   he will keep your life.*
The Lord will keep
*   your going out and your coming in*
*   from this time forth and for evermore.*

The poets contrast the glaring rays of the oriental noonday sun with the frost and chill of the moonlit night. The Lord will keep the faithful from all real evil.

Popular superstition has always maintained that the rays of the moon were injurious. The word "moonstruck" has found its way into the English vocabulary. The same idea was commonly held in the days of Jesus. When the Master came down from the mount of transfiguration, a man pleaded for mercy, explaining that he had a "lunatick" son, an epileptic. Jesus cured the victim, whose fit had exposed him to the worst accidents, falling into the fire and the water. Jesus is the Lord of life. After healing the boy, Jesus explained to his disciples that if they had faith, even as a tiny mustard seed, nothing would be impossible.

In the days of Jesus the feast of the new moon played an important role. It was a day of rejoicing, when special sacrifices were offered and the sound of trumpets was heard.

Sing aloud to God our strength;
shout for joy to the God of Jacob!
Sing, accompanied by drums;
pluck the sweet lyre and harp.
Sound the trumpet! Come to the
joyous celebrations at full moon,
new moon and all the other holidays!
For God has given us these times of joy;
they are scheduled in the laws of Israel.

The standard calendar was lunar. Had not God created the lesser light to rule the night, and assigned the moon to mark the months! So

> *Praise Him who made the heavenly lights,*
> *for His lovingkindness continues*
> *forever:*
> *The sun to rule the day, for His*
> *lovingkindness continues forever;*
> *And the moon and stars at night, for His*
> *lovingkindness continues forever!*

The moon has inspired both prose and poetry and stirred the imagination of man.

Almost three thousand years ago King David, the psalmist of Israel, wrote:

> *O Lord our God, the majesty and glory*
> *of Your name fills all the earth and*
> *overflows the heavens.*

When I look up into the night skies and
see the work of Your fingers—the
moon and the stars You have made—
I cannot understand how You can bother
with mere puny man, to pay any
attention to him!
And yet You have made him only a little
lower than the angels, and placed a
crown of glory and honor upon his
head.
You have put him in charge of everything
You made; everything is put under his
authority:
All sheep and oxen, and wild animals,
too,
The birds and fish, and all the life in the
sea.
O Jehovah, our Lord, the majesty and
glory of Your name fills the earth.

God sits above the circle of the earth; he
stretches out the heavens like a curtain, and
spreads them like a tent to dwell in. God is
the high and lofty One who inhabits eternity,
whose name is Holy. What is man that God
would be mindful of him? All the inhabitants
of the earth are like grasshoppers, and even
the great men of the world are brought to
naught. But God has crowned man with glory
and honor, and has given him dominion.

The following series of five pictures shows the
earth as photographed from Apollo 9

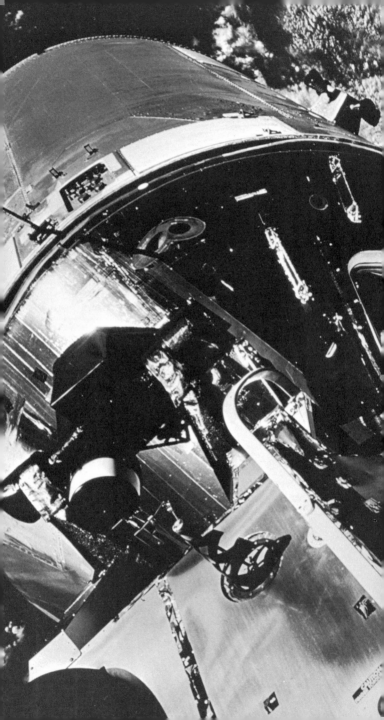

In Hebrew poetry the moon became a symbol of permanence.

> *In a vision You spoke to Your prophet and said, "I have chosen a splendid young man from the common people to be the king—He is My servant David! I have anointed him with My holy oil.*
> *I will steady him and make him strong.*
> *His enemies shall not outwit him, nor shall the wicked overpower him.*
> *I will beat down his adversaries before him, and destroy those who hate him.*
> *I will protect and bless him constantly and surround him with my love; he will be great because of Me.*
> *He will hold sway from the Euphrates River to the Mediterranean Sea.*
> *And he will cry to Me, 'You are my Father, my God, and my Rock of Salvation.'*
> *I will treat him as My firstborn son, and make him the mightest king in all the earth.*
> *I will love him forever, and be kind to him always; My covenant with him will never end. No, I will not break My covenant; I will not take back one word of what I said.*

*For I have sworn to David, (and a holy
God can never lie), that his dynasty will
go on forever, and his throne will continue to the end of time.
It shall be eternal as the moon, My
faithful witness in the sky!"*

The promise of God was fulfilled in Jesus
Christ. A new and better covenant was put
into effect, not written on tables of stone but
on the hearts of men. Every man would know
God, from the least to the greatest, for God
would forgive iniquity and remember sin no
more. This is the assurance received from
God, from him who

*gives the sun for light by day
and the fixed order of the moon
and the stars for light by night.*

The permanence of the covenant corres-
ponds to the permanence of the need.

*May the poor and the needy revere You
constantly, as long as the sun and moon
continue in the skies! Yes, forever!*

The promise of God and the need of man
meet in Jesus Christ.

*In his days righteousness will flourish
and peace abound, till the moon be
no more.*

Another note is heard in the book of Job:

*Dominion and fear are with God;
he makes peace in his high heaven.
Is there any number in his armies?
Upon whom does his light not arise?
How then can man be righteous before
God?
How can he who is born of woman be
clean?
Behold, even the moon is not bright
and the stars are not clean in his sight;
how much less man, who is a maggot,
and the son of man, who is a worm!*

The light of the moon is dark when contrasted with God who lives in unapproachable light.

Shakespeare wrote of "the chaste beams of the wat'ry moon," but Bildad, the friend of Job, felt that even the brightness of the moon is not pure in the sight of God. How much less, man who fails to reflect the glory of God.

The sympathy of Francis of Assisi embraced all nature. He cherished a feeling of

27

relationship with all of God's creation, addressing even inanimate creatures as brothers and sisters, including the sun and the moon. He had biblical precedent. In his exuberance the psalmist cries out:

> *Praise the Lord, O heavens! Praise Him*
> *from the skies!*
> *Praise Him, all His angels, all the armies*
> *of heaven.*
> *Praise Him, sun and moon, and all you*
> *twinkling stars.*
> *Praise Him, skies above. Praise Him,*
> *vapors high above the clouds.*
> *Let everything He has made give praise*
> *to Him!*
>
> *Praise Him down here on earth, you*
> *creatures of the ocean depths.*
> *Let fire and hail, snow, rain, wind and*
> *weather, all obey.*
> *Let the mountains and hills, the fruit*
> *trees and cedars,*
> *The wild animals and cattle, the snakes*
> *and birds,*
> *The kings and all the people, with their*
> *rulers and their judges,*
> *Young men and maidens, old men and*
> *children—*
> *All praise the Lord together. For He*
> *alone is worthy.*

Many poets have been deeply moved by the sight of the moon and have recorded their impressions. Milton, in *Paradise Lost*, describes a magnificent scene:

Now came still evening on, and twilight gray
Had in her sober livery all things clad;
Silence accompanied, for beast and bird,
They to their grassy couch, these to their nests,
Were slunk, all but the wakeful nightingale;
She all night long her amorous descant sung;
Silence was pleas'd: now glow'd the firmament
With living sapphires: Hesperus, that led
The starry host, rode brightest, 'til the moon
Rising in clouded majesty, at length
Apparent queen unveil'd her peerless light,
And o'er the dark her silver mantle threw.

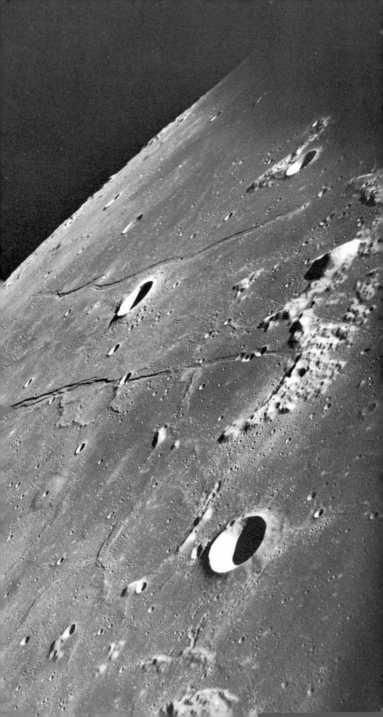

From the very beginning it was man's calling to have dominion over the realm in which he found himself. The control of nature is the task of man:

> *Thou hast given him dominion over the works of thy hands . . .*

To explore, to subdue, to conquer is the royal prerogative of man. Progress has been slow. It has taken thousands of years to reach the present stage of civilization and technology. Gradually the earth was conquered,

the oceans traversed, and the air penetrated. Man began to look into space.

Moon observation is an ancient art. In the second century B.C. Hipparchus led the way, followed by the great Ptolemy (A.D. 140). Not much happened until Tycho Brahe (1546-1601) took up the same topic once again, and Galileo peered through a telescope in 1610. The earliest moon map was drawn up in 1647. The names of Newton, Euler, and Laplace deserve mention. All these giants of the past prepared the way for moon exploration in our day.

The idea of space travel had been anticipated by seers and dreamers. It was over one hundred years ago that Jules Verne dreamed of submarines, aircraft, and television. His novels are dreams now come true.

In *From the Earth to the Moon*, published in 1865, the novelist wrote of launching a projectile which, like the Apollo, had three men aboard. The Frenchman chose a launching site about 100 miles from Cape Kennedy, Florida, near Tampa. December 1 was the date of the fictitious flight; December 11, its splashdown in the Pacific Ocean; and December 29, the day the capsule was to float to the surface. Actually, Apollo 8 was launch-

ed December 22, and the splashdown scheduled for December 27 in the Pacific.

Writing at a time when airplanes had not even been invented, Jules Verne estimated that his projectile would initially travel at about 25,000 miles an hour for the 238,833-mile journey. Apollo 8 began traveling at 24,200 miles an hour for the 225,000-mile flight. The French science fiction storyteller described his projectile as a cast-iron tube lined in aluminum, twelve feet high, with a base of fifty-four square feet and weighing 12,230 pounds. The Apollo crew compartment capsule was cone-shaped, twelve feet long and about thirteen feet wide. It had an aluminum alloy inner structure encased by a brazed stainless steel heatshield coated with plastic. It weighed 12,392 pounds. In Jules Verne's story the capsule orbited within twenty-five miles of the moon. The Apollo 8 crew described the moon's surface from a sixty-nine mile distance and photographed one area named for Jules Verne.

In fact, as much as 99.6 percent of the moon's surface has been photographed. Our information about the moon is remarkably accurate and detailed.

The mean distance between the earth and the moon is 238,860 miles. The moon's

diameter is 2159.9 miles, about one-fourth of the earth's diameter. The mass of the moon is only about one-hundredth of that of the earth, and the volume one-fiftieth. The temperature is highly undesirable from the human standpoint, and varies from 243° F to -261° F. Since atmosphere is almost nonexistent, absolute silence prevails on the moon.

The moon is a poor reflector. To begin with, the sun is 465,000 times as bright as the moon, and besides, the moon has an reflecting power of only approximately 11 percent. The gravity of the moon's surface exerts only about one-sixth of what we normally experience on earth. If an astronaut weighs 180 pounds on earth, he would weigh only 30 pounds on the moon. The enormous craters on the moon have always excited the imagination of man. Kepler, the famous German astronomer, believed that the craters on the moon were artificial, that they had been made by lunar creatures. One can only wonder what creatures he envisioned, since many craters are as wide as fifty miles from rim to rim. Craters of various dimensions are scattered over the entire surface of the moon.

The other striking features of the moon scenery are the so-called seas. It is generally assumed that they are the result of volcanic action, of lava which gradually cooled off and was then pitted by meteorites. The two forces which have shaped the features of the moon are impact and volcanism. It remains to be seen what the impact of man upon the moon will produce. Most puzzling to the astronomers are the strange narrow channels or valleys that look from a distance like river beds. Perhaps they are due to a faulting of the moon's crust. More than a thousand linear rills have been catalogued. In addition, there are some fifty rills that seem to meander aimlessly over the surface.

Another topic of debate has agitated the scientific community. Is the moon a globe burned out? Has the moon been hot at one time? The evidence seems to point in this direction. Basalt has been found on the surface of the moon and suggests a hot moon. Immediately the question arises: how did the moon get its heat?

It is common knowledge that the tides are directly related to the gravitational forces which the moon exerts upon the earth. The average interval between two successive high waters is 12 hours, 25 minutes. The range of tide varies on a daily basis. At the head of the Bay of Fundy the range of tide reaches fifty feet, while over most of the Mediterranean,

Helvelius' map of the full moon.

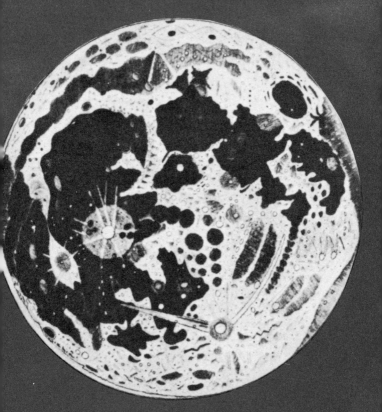

the range never exceeds two feet. It was not known until quite recently that the gravitational force of the moon affects not only the waters but also the land. The moon actually creates a tidal bulge in the surface of the earth which, like a wave, moves around the earth, always slightly ahead of the moon because the rotation of the earth is faster than that of the moon.

Centuries of study and research have culminated in our day and made space travel and moon exploration possible. The moon will be only the stepping stone to the universe. Exploration has just begun. It has taken man a long time to rise to the challenge of the Creator.

If the prophet Isaiah, 700 B.C., compared the nations of the world to a drop in the bucket, we have now become aware of the size of the bucket. The earth is so insignificant in terms of size that geocentric thinking seems preposterous and ridiculous. Yet the earth is the moral center of the universe.

The astronauts frequently refer to the "good old earth." Because there is no life on the moon, everything that makes life possible on earth takes on new value. Life, regardless of its nature, is not an accident. It is planned, created—a unique gift of God.

In the 17 century Johannes Hevelius, Odansk Astronomer to King John III Sobieski, took up the traditions of Nicolaus Copernicus. The etching presents a map of the surface of the moon, issued by Hevelius in his work SELENOGRAPHIA.

Even earth dwellers have become aware of the fact that our planet is only a global village. Seen from the moon, the earth appears in a new light. From outer space, little if anything of man's achievements on earth can be seen. Differences which seem significant, achievements which appear almost gigantic, vanish when seen from a lunar perspective. Perhaps man will yet gain a proper perspective upon himself when he sees himself from outer space. This seems to have been the experience of the astronauts.

The Apollo 8 crew closed its Christmas Eve special telecast by reading the following from the book of Genesis:

WILLIAM ANDERS—" *'In the beginning, God created the heaven and the earth.*

" 'And the earth was without form, and void; and darkness was upon the face of the deep. And the Spirit of God moved upon the face of the waters. And God said, Let there be light; and there was light. And God saw the light, that it was good, and God divided the light from the darkness.' "

JAMES LOVELL JR.—" *'And God called the light Day, and the darkness he called Night. And the evening and the morning were the first day. And God said, Let there be a firmament in the midst of the waters, and let*

stronauts Lovell, Anders, Borman.

it divide the waters from the waters. And God made the firmament, and divided the waters which were under the firmament from the waters which were above the firmament: and it was so. And God called the firmament Heaven. And the evening and the morning were the second day.' "

FRANK BORMAN—" *'And God said, Let the waters under the heavens be gathered together in one place, and let the dry land appear: and it was so. And God called the dry land Earth; and the gathering together of the waters called he Seas: and God saw that it was good.' "*

The Christmas Eve prayer, offered from lunar orbit by Col. Frank Borman and addressed to "people at St. Christophers—actually to people everywhere," should be echoed by every Christian:

"Give us, O God, the vision which can see thy love in the world in spite of human failure.

"Give us the faith to trust thy goodness in spite of our ignorance and weakness.

"Give us the knowledge that we may continue to pray with understanding hearts, and show us what each one of us can do to set forward the coming of the day of universal peace. Amen."

Isaac Watts (1674-1748) wrote:
> *Jesus shall reign where'er the sun*
> *Does his successive journeys run;*
> *His kingdom stretch from shore to shore,*
> *Till moons shall wax and wane no more.*

The comparison is apt, but only within limits. The day will come when
> *. . . the stars of the heavens and their*
> *constellations will not give*
> *their light;*
> *the sun will be dark at its rising*
> *and the moon will not shed its light.*

The moon will be confounded and the sun ashamed when the Lord shall reign. Their brightness will be eclipsed by the glory of God. In that day

> *No longer will you need the sun or moon*
> *to give you light, for the Lord your*
> *God will be your everlasting light, and*
> *He will be your glory.*

But before the dawn of this glorious era there will be cosmic turbulence, universal gloom; the earth will quake and the heavens tremble.

> *The sun and moon are obscured and*
> *the stars are hid.*

It is a time of judgment when the sun shall be turned to darkness and the moon to blood. Jesus predicted:

> *Immediately after the persecution of*
> *those days the sun will be darkened, and*
> *the moon will turn black, and the stars*
> *will seem to fall from the heavens, and*
> *the powers overshadowing the earth will*
> *be convulsed; then shall appear the sign*
> *of the Son of man in heaven.*

God is light. The first creative word was: Let there be light. Darkness was dispelled. Darkness and night are the symbols of evil, sin, and judgment. Jesus is the light of the world, and came to destroy the works of darkness. All of world history has been a mixture of light and darkness. It seems that often the powers of darkness prevail. Finally, once more the world will be plunged into the darkness of judgment, to be followed by the eternal triumph of light.

If the initial creative act concerns the light, if the moon is on the opening page of the Bible, the last reference to the moon is most appropriately found in the book of the Revelation of John. The eternal city of God

has no need of sun or moon to light it, for the glory of God and of the Lamb illuminate it.

It is not necessary to wait till that day to walk in the light of the Lamb. Jesus said,

I am the light of the world; he who follows me will not walk in darkness, but will have the light of life.

The earth as seen from the moon

CREDITS:
dust jacket: NASA
p. 7: Bettman Archive
p. 8: Oriental Institute, University of Chicago
p. 11: Bettman Archive
p. 13: photo by Harold M. Lambert
pp. 17-24: NASA, Apollo 9 flight
p. 30: NASA Apollo 8 flight
p. 33: Henry Schuman, Inc.
p. 34: George Allen and Unwin Ltd.
p. 39: NASA, Apollo 8 flight
pp. 40-41: Photograph by Harold M. Lambert
p. 49: NASA, Apollo 8 flight
p. 50: Photograph by Harold M. Lambert
p. 54, 56-58: NASA, Apollo 8 flight

Solutions for Creating the Learning Sp

T3-BLC-886

Reimagining
Literacy Through
Global Collaboration

Pernille Ripp

Solution Tree | Press

a division of

Solution Tree

Copyright © 2017 by Solution Tree Press

All rights reserved, including the right of reproduction of this book in whole or in part in any form.

555 North Morton Street
Bloomington, IN 47404
800.733.6786 (toll free) / 812.336.7700
FAX: 812.336.7790

email: info@SolutionTree.com
SolutionTree.com

Visit **go.SolutionTree.com/21stcenturyskills** to access materials related to this book.

Printed in the United States of America

20   19   18   17   16   1   2   3   4   5

Library of Congress Control Number: 2016954661

ISBN: 978-1-945349-28-7 (paperback)

Solution Tree
Jeffrey C. Jones, CEO
Edmund M. Ackerman, President

Solution Tree Press
President and Publisher: Douglas M. Rife
Editorial Director: Tonya Maddox Cupp
Managing Production Editor: Caroline Weiss
Senior Production Editor: Christine Hood
Senior Editor: Amy Rubenstein
Copy Chief: Sarah Payne-Mills
Copy Editor: Ashante K. Thomas
Proofreader: Jessi Finn
Text and Cover Designer: Abigail Bowen
Editorial Assistants: Jessi Finn and Kendra Slayton

To my mother, Nete Schmidt, who taught me that my dreams mattered, that my voice had power, and that the world was not something to hide from but instead something worth exploring.

Acknowledgments

As I teach, I am reminded every day of the vast world around us. Students come to us with an array of experiences, questions, and curiosities, and many of them stem from a deep fascination with the outside world. Others constantly influence us, whether or not we are aware of it, and I am no different. My work has been shaped by many great minds, both those whom I count as friends and colleagues and also those found through countless interactions with virtual strangers as I have collaborated, connected, and expanded my own horizons through social media. I am truly grateful to all who have shared their ideas over the years—those whose tweets or posts led me down my own rabbit hole as I realized that the world could be brought into our classrooms and that students should create for others.

To the original group of teachers who believed in the Global Read Aloud: thank you for believing in the project, spreading the word, and making it so much more than what I had ever envisioned. To those who have joined since then: your passion is what drives the project forward. To the authors whose books fuel the work I do: thank you for creating worlds that we can fall in love with, explore, and connect through.

To the educators who pushed me forward on this journey of sharing my work and my students' work with others—Dean Shareski, Tony Sinanis, Chris Wejr, Josh Stumpenhorst, Will Chamberlain, Shannon Miller, Jerry Blumengarten, and many more—thank you for seeing more in my work than I saw. To my edu-sisters—Kaye Henrickson, Leah Whitford, and Tammy Lind—your constant guidance, friendship, and support have made the biggest difference between good and great in my life. To all the other amazing educators

I connect with online: I am so grateful for every single interaction. To all the amazing educators in the Oregon School District: I am honored to be part of a district that puts kids first, no matter what.

To my family, those who continue to think that my crazy ideas are great and always have some of their own to share: I would not have the courage to spread my ideas were it not for you. To my one and only Brandon: thank you for asking, "Why don't you . . . " when it really mattered. To my amazing children, who talk about their dreams of the world and remind me that at my core, being a parent is the biggest job of all: this work is for you.

To the students I get to teach: your honesty, creativity, and questions are what drive this journey. Your expectations that literacy could be more, could be better, are what have shaped this entire book; I am so thankful I got to have a small part in your journey.

Solution Tree Press would like to thank the following reviewers:

Jenna Fanshier
Language Arts Teacher
Hesston Middle School
Hesston, Kansas

Angela Patterson
Fourth-Grade Team Teacher
Swanson Elementary School
Brookfield, Wisconsin

Taji Gibson
English Teacher
Bloomington High School
    North
Bloomington, Indiana

Katie Spear
Fourth- and Fifth-Grade
    Teacher
McKinley Elementary School
San Leandro, California

Samantha Harris
Reading Recovery® Teacher
    Leader
Alpine Independent School
    District
American Fork, Utah

Laurence Spring
Superintendent of Schools
Schenectady City School
    District
Schenectady, New York

Table of Contents

Chapter 3: Global Connections With an Authentic Audience 39

About the Author

 **Pernille Ripp** is a seventh-grade English language arts teacher in Oregon, Wisconsin, and a speaker, author, blogger, and passionate advocate for education. She is a Skype Master Teacher, Microsoft Innovative Educator Expert, and recipient of the 2015 WEMTA (Wisconsin Educational Media & Technology Association) Making IT Happen Award and the 2015 ISTE (International Society for Technology in Education) Award for Innovation in Global Collaboration. In 2010, Pernille founded Global Read Aloud, a worldwide literacy initiative that began with a simple goal in mind: to connect the world by reading the same book aloud simultaneously. From its humble beginnings, the Global Read Aloud has grown to connect more than two million students in different countries.

Pernille's research interest is in creating passionate literacy environments within the framework of U.S. education systems in order to help students fall in love with literacy again. She uses her own classroom as a laboratory and gathers ideas from the many educators she works with around the world. Pernille is the author of *Passionate Learners: How to Engage and Empower Your Students*, now in its second edition, and *Empowered Schools, Empowered Students: Creating Connected and Invested Learners*. Both books focus on creating learning spaces and communities where students thrive and all stakeholders are empowered and passionate about learning.

To learn more about Pernille's work, visit www.pernillesripp.com, or follow @pernilleripp on Twitter.

Foreword

By William M. Ferriter

Can I ask you a tough question? How many students in your classrooms are truly satisfied with the learning spaces you have created for them? If your students reflect the national average, the answer is bound to be discouraging. Fewer than four in ten high schoolers report being engaged in their classes, and students often list boredom as the primary reason for dropping out of school (Busteed, 2013). Over 70 percent of students who don't graduate report having lost interest by ninth grade and, worse yet, the majority of dropouts are convinced that motivation is all that prevented them from earning a diploma (Azzam, 2007).

These numbers are troubling for anyone passionate about schools. They indicate systemic failure on the part of practitioners to inspire learners and warn us of the immediate need to transform education—a warning that school leadership expert and series contributor Scott McLeod (2014) issues:

> If we truly care about preparing kids for life and work success—*we need schools to be different*. If economic success increasingly means moving away from routine cognitive work, schools need to also move in that direction. If our analog, ink-on-paper information landscapes outside of school have been superseded by environments that are digital and online and hyperconnected and mobile, our information landscapes inside of school also should reflect those shifts. If our students' extracurricular learning opportunities often are richer and deeper than what they experience in

their formal educational settings, it is time for us to
catch up.

Scott is right, isn't he? Our schools really do need to catch up if
they are going to remain relevant in a world where learning is more
important than schooling—and catching up can only start when we
are willing to rethink everything. We need to push aside the current norms defining education—that teachers are to govern, direct,
and evaluate student work; that mastering content detailed in pre-
determined curricula is the best indicator of student success; that
assessment and remediation are more important than feedback and
reflection; that the primary reason for investing in tools and technolo-
gies is to improve on existing practices. It's time to implement notions
that better reflect the complexity of the world in which we live.

That is the origin of this series. It is my attempt to give a handful
of the most progressive educators that I know a forum for detailing
what they believe it will take to *make schools different*. Each book
encourages readers to question their core beliefs about what meaningful teaching and learning look like in action. More important,
each title provides readers with practical steps and strategies for
reimagining their day-to-day practices. Here's your challenge: no
matter how unconventional these ideas, steps, and strategies may
seem at first, and no matter how uncomfortable they make you feel,
find a way to take action. There is no other way to create the learning spaces that your students deserve.

Introduction

I was born in a small town in the heart of Denmark called Bjerringbro. Surrounded by farm fields and enveloped in a community where it seemed like everybody knew me, I never imagined that I would become a teacher in the U.S. public school system. In fact, I never imagined I would become a teacher. That was for those who felt they had the power to change the world, and I most certainly did not feel that way.

When my mother got the opportunity to migrate to Wisconsin, I took a chance and went along, not quite knowing how long I would stay or what I would do. I was eighteen, newly graduated from junior college, and not quite sure what to do with myself. I had left my country behind, and I felt so lost. It took years to find my place, to feel at home, and to feel like I was no longer lost. Becoming a teacher was a large part of the journey to find out who I was.

When I became a fourth-grade teacher, I knew that regardless of the path that led students to my classroom, they should never feel lost like I had, but instead, they should find ways to create connections with everyone around them. They would connect with not only those they interacted with daily but also those outside our Wisconsin classroom. I knew that their dreams for themselves and the world they live in deserved a larger audience than just me. Therefore, I set out to create a globally connected classroom, and for many years, this has continued to be my mission: to create a classroom where students truly feel that they are citizens of the world, that their voices matter, and that what they do matters not just to each other but to people they will never meet in person.

While my initial dream of global citizenry was lofty, my students' desire proved bigger than my dreams. My students wanted to have shared experiences so they could discuss books, their writing, and their expertise and reflect with other students who did not lead the same lives or share the same experiences. So we decided to blog. They wanted to use Skype (www.skype.com) to speak to experts, other classrooms, and anyone else who could add something to our learning. It was not that they wanted to learn more technology; they wanted to connect.

So, I stopped scheduling New Tool Thursdays and instead asked my students what we could do with the tools we already knew how to use. Soon, my students had ideas to share that started to change the way we used our literacy time together. It is from these ideas that the seeds of this book were planted and then grew. My students wanted more than what I was offering, so I had to find a way to provide them with opportunities to collaborate, create, and find others to become part of their literacy journey.

I had to create a global literacy experience, even if I was not sure exactly what that entailed. Adding an audience to their writing or engaging in discussions with classrooms far from us would ensure that they saw the greater purpose of what reading and writing could do for them as world citizens, rather than allowing them to treat their literacy work as just another assignment.

While my students have since changed from eight- and nine-year-olds to twelve- and thirteen-year-olds, my purpose for teaching has not changed. I still want to create an experience for students in which they see their own ideas extend beyond our classroom. I want them to realize the reach they can have and also how other students can influence them in order to explore their place in the world. As part of developing their unique *literacy identity*, or how they view themselves as readers, writers, and speakers, they must understand their larger place in the world.

I hope this book will provide you with inspiration to start or further your own journey to becoming, and helping your students become, global citizens. You do not need to focus on technology; instead, expand the world of literacy your students function within—that change can start today. We can create classrooms where our students know that once they leave they will never feel lost in the world because they have experienced what it means to be connected. We can create classrooms that make schools different for all of the students we have yet to teach. We can create classrooms where what they create matters. The journey starts now.

Chapter 1
Global Collaboration for Literacy

"Did you see what they said?" One of my students approached me with his laptop computer open to the feedback he received on a picture book play the class recently performed, which was videotaped and then shared with others around the world. "This kindergartner thinks I'm funny. . . . That's pretty awesome."

As he walked away, showing his friend the comments and beaming at the news, I silently thanked the kindergarten teacher for signing up her class to be our audience and leaving us feedback on Google Forms (www.google.com/forms). This student was not alone in his glee. Some students were still in awe that others had seen them perform; others simply smiled, while some were downright indignant. "How dare they tell me I need to have more eye contact," one student exclaimed.

Nestled within their seventh-grade dreams, and straining against the constraints of our forty-five-minute class periods, is a desire to create for others, which has transformed not just our literacy experiences but also the very essence of learning itself. With minimal time, minimal tools, and sometimes even just a minimal idea, seventh-grade English has come to mean learning with the world whenever possible. No longer does this class just cover the basics of reading, writing, grammar, and speaking, but instead, it offers opportunities for all students to learn about the outside world, make connections with virtual strangers, and discover that their ideas and dreams matter to others. Welcome to our global literacy classroom!

The Global Literacy Classroom

In his article "The Six Ts of Effective Elementary Literacy Instruction," education researcher Richard Allington (2002) outlines students' literacy needs in order to create successful and effective literacy experiences. He finds that for students to have rich literacy experiences, they not only need the six components—time, texts, teach, talk, tasks, and tests—but they also need highly invested and inventive teachers who focus on their own development as practitioners.

Allington (2002) writes, "Good teachers, effective teachers, manage to produce better achievement regardless of which curriculum materials, pedagogical approach, or reading program is selected." This statement is part of the global literacy classroom's backbone; it is not a curriculum or a process to be followed, but rather a way for educators to infuse their pre-existing literacy curriculum with more global opportunities. It is meant to entice student engagement and create more meaningful learning opportunities that further deepen students' knowledge of themselves as readers, writers, speakers, and even human beings. It rests on three foundational needs of creating literacy experiences in which students collaborate with others, create for others, and connect with others to understand and enhance their own literacy experiences.

Students collaborating around a single purpose is nothing new. People have always had a place for collaboration within their communities, which has spurred great inventions, such as the foundation for the U.S. public school system. This school system traces its origins to a religious group in Massachusetts who realized that if they educated the masses, society as a whole would benefit (Boston Latin School, n.d.). Created on the foundation of working together, it is therefore fitting that since its inception, the public school experience has included collaboration as a pillar of its system as teachers provide learning structures that prepare students to be active members of society. Within the curriculum, educators have created opportunities for students not to learn in isolation, but rather to use the school experience to find their place in the world.

The ease with which we can access connections and collaborations has increased as our technology continues to advance, yet the idea of collaboration to become more knowledgeable is a foundation of our society and can be traced back hundreds of years to the creation of think tanks in the mid-1700s (Mendizabal, 2010). Coming together for a shared purpose is not revolutionary, yet the notion of global collaboration to enhance literacy instruction has received more attention with the advent of technology entering our classrooms. This technology infiltration has heightened the need for student awareness, technological proficiency, and also technological access in order to create classroom experiences that mirror the experiences students will have once they graduate.

We live in a time in which students are no longer limited to contained experiences within our classrooms, and teachers in isolated locations can be part of global collaborative networks using whichever tools they can access (Ripp, 2015). By becoming connected through literacy work, students can take part in projects, such as creating informational picture books for younger students, becoming teachers of various content to classrooms around the world, or even taking part in research projects that other students facilitate.

The benefits that this affords them on a global scale cannot be ignored; students can now have an incredible literacy experience through the impact of others' impressions and ideas that enable them to explore their own identities as creators. This allows them to further explore not just *how* they read and write but also *why* they read and write. While we are the primary teachers for students who enter our schools, our students can and should be connected to other students around the world, which provides them with literacy experiences that could not be concocted by a single teacher.

As Thomas L. Friedman (2005) writes in his book *The World Is Flat*, "You have to trust that the dots will somehow connect in your future" (p. 318). Therefore, if we think of what we teach as dots in the journey of all learners, we must provide students with opportunities to connect those dots to the dots that surround them in the outside world. Having access to tools that allow us to easily expand our projects and our learning beyond the four walls of the classroom is thus a cornerstone of the global literacy classroom—protected and cultivated as part of what sets schools and learning experiences apart from one another.

Technology access and use are not the only determining factors in creating a successful global literacy classroom; the very purpose of what we create, the experiences we are immersed in, as well as whom we create for become essential components as well. If we take care in creating opportunities that embrace the philosophy of the global literacy experience, one in which students are given opportunities to collaborate and create with others and for others, then students will experience authentic opportunities to see and understand how their own identities as readers or writers can shape their place in the world.

Authentic Global Collaboration

Global collaboration—the term itself has become an education phrase often heard in professional development as well as at conferences. Yet what does it really mean? Is global collaboration simply sending out a message on a social media platform highlighting student work, or does it go beyond that? As someone who has been immersed in global collaboration for several years, I believe that *authentic* global collaboration includes not just a product but also a reciprocal process between collaborators. As James Surowiecki (2004) writes in *The Wisdom of Crowds*, "A large group of diverse individuals will come up with better and more robust forecasts and make more intelligent decisions than even the most skilled 'decision maker'" (p. 22).

Therefore, advocating for students creating in groups, or at least not in a solitary vacuum, makes sense when we think of what students must experience within our literacy curriculum. Their learning process is enhanced when we expand the notion of what collaboration really looks like. So while showcasing student work through something like a classroom website or a tweet is a step, it does not encompass the term's full meaning. Rather, authentic global collaboration revolves around the following four key features.

1. We go beyond product sharing and offer a give-and-take between collaborating parties.

2. We create the product or process with the intention of sharing it with others.

3. We find the audience or purpose of the process mostly outside our school.

4. We collaborate to add value to the product, thus causing the learning and exploration process to change.

These are not the only features of an authentic globally collaborative project, but they are necessary to create the type of experience in which we hope to immerse our students, an experience that adds value to instruction and whose inherent value the student experience compounds. It should, consequently, become an experience that expands the core learning by adding a deeper layer that would be impossible to reach if it were not for collaboration itself.

While it may seem that creating a global literacy classroom is limited to those with technology access, this is not accurate. Instead, one must have a desire to create connections with others through technology or traditional methods. You can create with the world through just one device or portal, and the portal does not have to be electronic. Some of the most powerful connections made in classrooms have been in situations when students received packages through the mail, a service that has been in place since 1775 (United States Postal Service, n.d.). Using technology tools simply makes the process easier.

Realizing that the four key features of an authentic global experience will change the very work performed allows educators to change the way they plan and implement lessons in their classrooms. Moving global collaboration away from just sharing student work to a means of providing an audience with a way to communicate and also learn about a tool that shapes the work process itself allows students to become connected on a more personal level. Yes, they will explore content and knowledge through connections, but these shared learning opportunities also help students develop empathy and understanding for cultures outside their own.

By immersing students in global literacy experiences, they no longer feel a connection just to their immediate community; instead, they see themselves as part of something bigger, which should spark curiosity and awe as they grow into adulthood and realize the impact they can have on the world. For example, while immersed in the Global Read Aloud and listening to the book *Out of My Mind* by Sharon Draper, my students were inspired to create a public service announcement (PSA) video to stop using the word *retarded* in a derogatory way in our school and elsewhere. Knowing that audiences outside of our school would potentially be inspired to rethink their language gave them a sense of urgency to do better and drove their further investment in the project.

As Angela Maiers says, "The greatest gap in American education is the underestimation of student genius and their capacity to contribute. We don't see students as agents of impact" (as cited in Snelling, 2016, p. 27). Students can and should have an impact on the world outside their classrooms; we can offer them that opportunity.

Adding a global component to our literacy curriculum is a natural fit. After all, much of what we do in a literacy curriculum is an exploration of one's own literacy identity cemented in the process of becoming a reader, writer, and speaker. Adding authentic global opportunities within the framework of what we already do is not just attainable but of urgent importance. We are in charge of educating tomorrow's adults, and those adults need to be literate not just in the traditional sense but also in the global sense. We should create and embrace learning opportunities that allow students to explore other cultures, other mindsets, and other worldviews. And since our instructional days typically do not carve out standalone time for such exploration, we must find a way to weave it into what we already do.

From Hallway Displays to the World

When you walk into many schools, student work is on display for visitors to peruse and admire. Yet, while sharing student work is a first step toward creating a more collaborative and connected environment, it is not enough. Arming students with the knowledge that their final product is public, schools often use the hallway display as a way to enhance quality and inspire engagement, yet the reverse may be true.

Students accustomed to these displays develop a sort of numbness to the displays themselves. When we tell students that their work is going up in a hallway, it is simply not enough to enhance the connection or commitment to the work—not when they can reach for a device, create something through an app, and then share it with an audience that can respond almost instantaneously. No longer do hallway displays for the same audience year after year inspire students to think deeper, create more, or even revise better. Stapling projects to a hallway wall is not enough for students to thoroughly engage with what they are creating. Simply put, the walls of our schools have become the new refrigerator doors—a tool for display but not one that creates further engagement.

Therefore, it is essential that the opportunity to share student work goes beyond the actual classroom or school walls and into the wider world. For example, my students write a blog using the platform Kidblog (http://kidblog.org/home). This journey as writers with a global platform is revered and protected within our classroom, and I use it as a way for students to realize the impact of their words on an outside audience.

When the students' blogging journey begins, I ask our staff to be the first to leave comments. Students get a taste of what it feels like to have their writing out in public, and staff members get a chance to get to know the students better. Yet, the novelty of that wears off quickly, as it should; it is very similar to stapling their papers to the wall.

When a stranger, usually an educator or a fellow student, leaves a comment asking questions and striking up a conversation, that is when my students see the power of the blogging platform. Having these comments to consider as they shape their own writing allows students to hone their message, revise their work, and consider future audiences for anything they write. They would never consider these things were it not for the blogging platform. Knowing that their posts can potentially be read and shared by others inspires students not only to work harder at what they are creating but also to think of how someone else might respond to their message.

Blogging with my students and reaching more than six hundred thousand unique visitors across six years has taught me that students no longer yearn to write for the people they see every day; instead, they yearn to find a larger audience, much like the one they find on their own if they write *fan fiction* (stories based on characters established by another author) or participate in any online communities or social media. Our job as educators is to take that desire and funnel it into our own projects. Whenever we undertake collaborative projects in order to create a global literacy environment, the bottom line is the inherent value in collaboration, not that it looks good in our lesson planner.

While most of my students have been blogging for a long time, blogging can still be a new phenomenon from year to year. So, every year, I re-explore the medium of blogging with my classes to make sure it still fits my students' needs. The reason we invest our time year after year is because blogging provides students with a portal to share their views and opinions with the rest of the world. It also provides them with a protected space where they can explore their identities and share the pieces that define them with a larger audience around the globe.

The Benefits of Global Collaboration

Speak to educators who have participated in global literacy collaboration, and you will soon notice a pattern in their responses; the success that their students feel is apparent, as is the deeper engagement the process creates for both students and themselves as part of a greater community of peers. These two factors of success are some of many reasons why educators choose to invest their time and energy in creating and joining global opportunities for students. Yet these are not the only benefits to students. Some others include a renewed sense of purpose, pride, and community, and a renewed understanding of technology and the long-term implications of their digital footprint.

Renewed Sense of Purpose

Students feel that what they are creating actually matters because their audience is not just their families and teachers. When another student or class finds value in their work, it starts to transform their sense of purpose. Students see the real effects that their creation can have on others, and it spurs them forward. One example of this can be found in the story of Josh, whose name I changed to protect his identity.

Josh was not a typical student; he struggled with his emotions and how to work through frustrations, often becoming visibly angry in school. He sometimes resorted to yelling or hitting objects in order to process his anger. While his classmates knew Josh as a friendly and smart student, they also knew his struggles, which meant that he would often share how alone he felt, as many students found him too strange to have as a friend. In his first blog post, Josh wrote that he decided to introduce himself to the world by sharing a story he had written for a choice-driven narrative assignment. After he hit Publish, his story was shared through Twitter (https://twitter.com) using the hashtag #Comments4Kids to see if any other students would comment.

The very next day, Josh came to school bursting with pride. He had seen the positive comments that other classrooms in North America left for his story and even read one that said they were eagerly awaiting the rest of the tale. Not only could he not wait to write more so as not to leave his audience waiting, but he had a different air about him. He realized that some students now only knew him as Josh the Writer, rather than Josh the Angry Child. Through that moment on his blog, he could be what he had always longed to be: a kid just like everybody else.

Renewed Sense of Pride

When students receive positive feedback or even constructive criticism from strangers, it is as if everything their teachers, and possibly even parents, have said through the years finally falls into place. As illustrated by the story of Josh and his sense of pride at being an author in the eyes of others, students who participate in a collaborative literacy process become more invested in and have more sense of pride in and ownership of their work.

One writing project my seventh graders create is a nonfiction picture book for kindergartners or first graders. They use Skype to speak to students in this age group to ask them as many questions as they can, gathering their market research and infusing their newfound knowledge into the final product. Once the books have been created in Google Slides (www.google.com/slides), students then share them with an audience of the targeted age group in classrooms around the world. My class invites other classes to read their books and leave feedback through Google Forms (sometimes teacher facilitated); and finally, these classes share their feedback with my student authors.

While many students have heard from teachers that they need to work on spelling or punctuation, hearing it from a six-year-old really makes a difference. Year after year, I witness the effect of this kind of feedback on my students' future work, as students often weave the feedback into their own learning goals. Throughout the year, they may refer to it as well and tell each other that they really need to work on something because "this kid" said so. I watch in amazement when students who don't seem to care about much get excited about the feedback they receive from others, and then, more importantly, decide to incorporate that feedback into their learning projects, extending the learning into something inherently more meaningful to them as individuals, not just students.

Renewed Sense of Community

Students yearn to see where they fit into the world and often crave attention and notice; this is part of what ties them together. We need only look at the popularity of Instagram (www.instagram.com) among students to know that figuring out a place in the world and where they fit is of great importance to them. They often define themselves through the reactions of others. So, why not harness this desire as a way to strengthen your classroom community? By participating as a unit in a global project, students begin to understand what makes their classroom unique and the strengths of their immediate community. They start to distill the essence of their togetherness when they have to introduce their class to others or determine what to share.

For example, my fourth graders completed a collaborative community project with a third-grade special education class in New York. Each class created a video showcasing its community both inside and outside of school and then created a care package to go with the video. As students prepared for their video speeches, they became aware of how different their community might be from others. When they watched the third graders' class video, they were surprised at how much those students' experiences differed from their own, but they were even more aware of what tied them together.

Because students had to cater their presentation to a specific audience, they carefully selected what they chose to highlight. While the content of what they shared was important, students also discovered that every word mattered, as did how they spoke those words. By understanding their own skills as storytellers, students discovered how the way we tell a story can affect the intended audience. This is the essence of what it means to be in a global literacy environment; students feel that they know who they are but also gain an awareness of how their own identities translate to the rest of the world.

Renewed Understanding of Technology

Depending on a school's location and resources, access to technology can vary greatly from school to school. However, no matter what kind of technology tools a school offers, students typically know more about these tools than the teachers. Teachers should tap into this knowledge and expertise. Ask students what tools they already use at home, and encourage them to see that they can use these tools to communicate with others rather than just share about themselves.

Renewed Understanding of the Digital Footprint

One new component of curriculum for many educators is digital citizenry. With 92 percent of teens reporting that they go online daily (Lenhart, 2015), we have an immense responsibility, from the early years, to educate students on how to use digital tools safely and with respect and dignity. Teaching students how to safely and skillfully navigate and use the Internet has become vital as we educate the adults of the future. While some students already understand that what they share online creates a digital footprint of sorts, many still do not recognize the long-term ramifications that this digital footprint can have.

According to the American Academy of Child and Adolescent Psychiatry (AACAP), teens think about their actions differently than adults do. The teenage brain develops in such a way that most decisions are "guided more by the amygdala and less by the frontal cortex" (AACAP, 2011). This means that teens often make decisions without as much forethought or reflection as we would expect. This matters when students are developing their online persona and is part of the reason educators should create or join authentic global projects— so students can develop a habit of positive interactions online.

Engaging students in global collaborative projects means that they see the footprint creation as well as the effect their online interactions can have on other people. While these experiences may not steer them away from all poor decisions, they can help shape the very conversations we have about what it means to be active online and how those online personas can impede or enhance their lives both inside and outside the classroom.

Global Literacy Experiences

One strength of teaching literacy is that so many activities we already do lend themselves incredibly well to global collaboration, thus taking the preexisting connections that students hopefully feel to our literacy environment and extending those connections to the world. By incorporating global collaboration into the pillars of literacy instruction, such as read alouds, book discussions, and research writing, we can create immersive learning opportunities in which students feel that their literacy identity matters not only to their teachers but also to the outside world. This is important if we want to create learning that is relevant and engaging. Students must see beyond our classroom walls to know that the self-discovery they experience within our curriculum will lead to them feeling more established within the context of our global society.

One teacher who exemplifies what it means to create a relevant and engaging global literacy project is Sandy Wisneski, a lead teacher in Ripon, Wisconsin. She participated in a project called Kids' Comic Con's Comics Club International with her sixth-grade students. Together with comic artist Alex Simmons from the Bronx, New York, her class learned how to plan, write, and then create comic books that answer the driving question, How would you use superpowers to improve a global problem?

Throughout the project, Simmons helped students as they shared examples of their work and discussed their progress, while offering suggestions and guidance. However, these students were not alone; students in Ireland and Senegal participated in the project at the same time. They used Google Hangouts (https://hangouts.google .com) to discuss their work with other artists around the world.

Each group of students created its own original comic book character illustrations, story ideas, and more, and the program culminated in a special international exhibition of the students' work. When asked how the program enhanced her existing instruction, Sandy Wisneski said:

> The project enhanced learning with real-world experts on the topic we were working on, as well as expanding our classroom walls working with classes from around the world, allowing us to use digital citizenship skills in a real-life setting. Students felt that they were valued because an expert was willing to give them the time to meet with the class and offer his skills and knowledge. The students also gained information from people [whom] I was unable to bring into the classroom, since we are a smaller rural community, and cultural awareness took on new meaning connecting with classes internationally. (personal communication, March 28, 2016)

Seeing the inherent value of global collaboration is what inspires many to join the Global Read Aloud, a project I created in 2010, which has connected more than two million students on six continents. This simple project, which centers on sharing a book read aloud during a set time period and then using technology to connect, is based on something many literacy teachers already incorporate in some way: the simple read aloud.

We should not underestimate the importance of reading aloud, even with older students. As research shows, "Read alouds . . . stimulate curiosity in children as they are invited into a safe environment to marvel at the concepts being presented" (Harvey, 1998, as cited in Wadsworth, 2008, p. 1). Knowing how important wonder and curiosity are for creative problem solving, we must embrace literacy elements that help students develop curiosity, and the read aloud helps us do that. Furthermore, in the report *Becoming a Nation of Readers*, the authors state, "The single most important activity for building the knowledge required for eventual success in reading is reading aloud to children" (Anderson, Hiebert, Scott, & Wilkinson, 1985, p. 23).

The importance of read alouds does not change, even as students grow older, affording educators a unique opportunity to take a known entity and turn it into something more meaningful. Therefore, taking this cornerstone of best literacy practice and adding the component of global collaboration makes sense because books naturally create connections between people who otherwise might have a hard time finding commonalities.

Much like Sandy Wisneski incorporated learning opportunities for her students through a known writing process, we must seek opportunities to further the existing curriculum to make it more engaging and meaningful for all students. We can accomplish this by joining or creating globally collaborative projects.

There are three paths to becoming part of collaborative opportunities: (1) join a preexisting project, (2) create a project with a partner, or (3) create your own project. Whichever path you take is up to you; all three have value, and often one leads to another. In fact, using all three paths throughout the school year can lead to a rich learning opportunity for students, which greatly expands who they are as learners and human beings.

Throughout the year, my students join preexisting projects, collaborate on projects with staff members within the Oregon School District where I work, and create their own projects as needed to fit within the curriculum we are exploring. All three paths add tremendous value to our classroom, and these experiences are necessary for us to create a global literacy environment. We will explore these three paths in the next chapter.

Reflection Questions

Before moving on to chapter 2, answer the following questions to reflect on this chapter.

1. What are you already doing to create connections beyond your own classroom?

2. To what kinds of technology tools do you have access?

3. What will your students gain from becoming more connected to the world?

4. What will you gain from these experiences?

5. How will students take ownership over their digital footprint as they share with others?

Chapter 2
Three Paths to Global Collaboration

I remember our first Skype call vividly—my fourth graders were eagerly sitting on the carpet waiting for the call to begin, sheets with questions clutched in their hands. We were as prepared as we could be; now the only question was whether the technology would work. Finally, after a few intense minutes of a black screen, the computer started to ring, and soon a face popped up on the screen. "Hello, everyone. I hear you may have a few questions for me."

My students' eyes lit up, and their hands shot into the air; they were more than ready to speak to the author, Adam Gidwitz, after reading his book in class. After our thirty-minute Skype call, a student approached me.

"Mrs. Ripp," he said with a huge grin on his face, "I thought writing was boring, but now I wonder how I can become an author. Maybe someday I can do that."

All I could think was that perhaps bringing others into our learning environment might just be the change that my students needed to become more invested. And I was certainly right! Several years later, my classes have logged five hundred thousand Skype miles, and my students no longer wonder whether the technology will work but, instead, with whom else they can learn. We do not just *do* literacy, we *live* it through every connection we make and every collaboration we attempt.

There are three distinct paths to global collaboration: (1) join a pre-existing project, (2) create a project with a partner, or (3) create your own project. Each of these paths presents its own set of benefits and challenges in the classroom. However, before you begin your journey into global collaboration, there are several things you must consider.

Before You Join or Create

One thing to consider before you venture into global collaboration is to make sure your students are ready to work with others. While we often assume that student community develops no matter what, we must be vigilant about the *type* of environment that develops. Students of different ages bring various challenges to creating community, yet creating a literacy classroom where students feel empowered to speak up, share their voice, and feel that what they have to say matters is paramount to globally collaborative projects' success. Dennis Harper (2003, as cited in Soundout [2015]) writes, "Student voice is giving students the ability to influence learning to include policies, programs, contexts and principles."

Providing ample opportunities for students to shape the very curriculum we teach is something we must do as an investment in the learning community. Without a solid foundation of student voices, you will not see as much change in how global literacy experiences impact your students for the better. Simply put, students must feel they have something worth sharing with the world for these experiences to be meaningful.

This foundation for a strong community should develop when we give students more voice and the tools to help plan their learning; however, this community is not guaranteed to happen. Therefore, it is important that we know how connected students feel to each other and how they interact with others before we bring in outsiders.

Student Readiness to Work With Others

You can assess student readiness in several ways. You might engage students in classroom challenges that center on a common purpose, such as a challenge to build a tower using certain materials. Can students accomplish such a task in a respectful way rather than in a way that creates strife? The answer to this question can guide your assessment of their readiness to collaborate outside the classroom. You might also consider incorporating Mystery Skype calls into your schedule. This geographical location guessing game allows students to practice problem solving and on-the-spot critical thinking without the teacher's guidance, which is an incredible way to develop the skills needed for a solid community. (Visit http://bit.ly/2dIjZ56 to learn more about Mystery Skype.)

Questions You Should Ask

Once you feel that students are ready, it's time to consider the other aspects of joining or creating a global collaborative project. Here are a few questions to ponder as you prepare.

- Which areas of literacy will this project influence?
- How much time can you devote to the project?
- What are your preferred digital or analog tools?
- Do students have a say in what you share?
- What are you hoping to accomplish from participating in this global project?

As previously mentioned, there are three paths to global collaboration: (1) join a preexisting project, (2) create a project with a partner, or (3) create your own project. Following is an explanation of each path so you can see what fits best for your students.

Tips for Joining a Preexisting Project

One of the easiest ways to get students to connect is to join a preexisting global project. Often, all you have to do is sign up and then follow directions. A community is already present to support and guide you, and you can make connections swiftly and efficiently. Following are a few preexisting global projects geared toward literacy, selected due to their global scope, ease of participation, and successful years of experience. (Visit **go.SolutionTree.com/21stcenturyskills** to access live links to the websites mentioned in this book.)

- **Global Read Aloud** (www.theglobalreadaloud.com) is a worldwide literacy initiative in which teachers read aloud a selected text within a set six-week period (usually starting in October) and then use whatever tools they have to connect with other participants. Book choices range from picture books to high school–level books.

- **International Dot Day** (www.thedotclub.org) typically occurs around September 15 and invites teachers and students to make dots to launch a creative journey. The activities range from simple watercolor and crayon creations to K–12 celebrations to days of community service.

- **Projects by Jen** (http://projectsbyjen.com/calendar.html) offers ongoing online projects created specifically for the prekindergarten through sixth-grade teacher; however, there's an option to choose Other for grade level. Each project lasts approximately one month and fosters collaboration across subjects. Each project meets several of the International Society for Technology in Education's student standards as well as many of the National Governors Association Center for Best Practices and the Council of Chief State School Officers' Common Core standards.

- **International Literacy Day** (www.literacyworldwide .org/ild) occurs on September 8 each year and focuses attention on worldwide literacy needs. Participating classrooms receive a free activity kit to help students learn about literacy's impact on a different country each year. All age levels are encouraged to participate in this worldwide literacy celebration.

- **Save Our Rhinos** (https://saveourrhinos.wikispaces .com) is a year-round initiative for grades K–12 that raises awareness of the dire rhino-poaching situation in South Africa. A toy rhino visits a class for approximately two weeks before moving on to another class. Five unique African stuffed rhinos have been sent with a journal in five different directions around the world to visit classrooms, and each class contributes a page in the project wiki. Most participants have been in K–6 classrooms, so it would be wonderful to have some older classes tackle this project on a deeper level.

Joining a preexisting global collaboration means that most of the work is done for you. In the case of a project like the Global Read Aloud, there is plenty of wiggle room to adapt it to fit your own unique needs and situation. However, you must follow certain guidelines. Many educators who have chosen to be part of global projects do a combination of preexisting activities as well as invent their own opportunities to ensure they meet the needs and desires of their students. Teachers who have been part of preexisting global projects often report that these projects have added immense value to their literacy classrooms by energizing their students to dream bigger and fueling their desire to create for others, not just for themselves and the teacher.

Tips for Creating With a Partner

Creating a project with a partner is another way to add a global component to your literacy instruction. Whether this means asking the teacher across the hall or someone else you are already familiar with is up to you. What matters is that you are not alone in the journey and have the support of someone you trust as you try to add a new dimension to your instruction.

There are two main ways that partnerships can work: (1) create together and (2) create for each other. The scope and focus of the project should fit both parties' needs. Partnerships between two different age groups can evolve into mentor-and-mentee relationships, whereas partnerships between similar age groups can evolve into a shared creative process. While many steps in creating or joining a project are similar to those you undergo when you are by yourself, having a trusted partner gives you the distinct benefit of having someone with whom to plan, navigate pitfalls, and evaluate. It becomes a joint venture instead of a solo one, which sometimes provides the incentive needed for students to create their own projects.

This partnership idea is what caused eighth-grade students from Maple Lake, Minnesota, to become writing partners with a group of eighth-grade students in Seoul, South Korea. Technology integration-ist Beth Haglin supported this community partnership by acting as the project's facilitator for the two teachers involved. She met with the teachers to determine their goals, which were for their students to practice effective communication skills and reflect on their self-selected reading texts. Both teachers were interested in the benefits of a global connection, but they had not tried anything like this before.

Haglin assisted the two teachers with using the technology, aligning their goals, and communicating with the teacher in Seoul whenever questions and issues arose. When asked whether global collaboration is important to education, she responded in the affir-mative, saying:

> I think it requires a mindshift, from covering stan-dards in the ways we always have, to including this type of experience along the way. Why not meet the standards *and* begin to know and care about peo-ple different from ourselves? Moreover, students can

begin to realize that, in some ways, we aren't all that different from one another. (B. Haglin, personal communication, March 29, 2016)

Having someone share your journey can sometimes make all the difference, but don't forget that this person does not have to come from your own school for a collaboration to be successful.

Tips for Creating Your Own Project

If you are feeling inspired and are ready to try something by yourself, or you cannot find a project that seems to fit your dreams, then it's time to create your own global project. It doesn't have to be anything large; it can be between you and one other class, or it can involve your class and many others. The scope and depth are up to you. The immense benefit of creating your own project is that you can shape it to fit your needs—you determine the timeline as well as the final product.

Such was the case for second-grade teacher Heather Simpson in Chatham, Ontario, Canada, when she created the Global Book Project. This yearlong project focused on students ages six to ten creating and sharing ebooks on six different topics: (1) their country and landform, (2) buildings, (3) celebrations, (4) food, (5) recreation, and (6) animals. Simpson's students collaborated with students in Australia, Bahrain, China, Germany, Malaysia, Panama, Russia, and the United States.

Simpson reached out to a few educators who already followed her on Twitter to ask whether they would be interested in participating in a project with her class. She shared the basic guidelines, and they started the ebook creation process, with the final products shared through Dropbox (www.dropbox.com) and Twitter. Students not only wrote the books; they also included sound files, which was a great way for students to experience different accents and languages. Some participating classrooms also shared videos, letters, and packages to further the connection.

With a focus on multiple literacy requirements, students have practiced developing inquiry questions for their book topics and learned how to research and synthesize information through their reading. They have developed their writing and technology skills using Book Creator (www.redjumper.net/bookcreator) to produce each book. They also have developed their collaborative skills through small-group work while creating something that the whole class will share. In addition, students have developed skills in comparing and contrasting, asking and answering questions, recording learned information, and using charts and maps.

Students weren't just meeting curricular requirements; this project's true beauty lies in the deep connections students forged with participating classes. The project truly shaped their experiences by offering them an authentic audience and purpose as they mastered their literacy skills. Simpson's students refer to the other participants as their friends, display these students' photos in their classroom, and now no longer think twice when it comes to connecting with others through Twitter and Skype. It is not just the students, however, who benefited from this global project. Simpson reports:

> It has made me more comfortable connecting with other teachers. I have gained new perspectives and learned much more about different parts of the world. I have been able to learn from all the great teachers involved with this project and have strengthened my [professional learning network]. It has made me want to seek out more global opportunities for my students. (personal communication, March 28, 2016)

Simpson offers the following advice if you want to participate in a long-term collaboration.

- **Invite people directly:** People are more likely to participate if they feel they are really wanted and if they are asked specifically to be involved in a project.

- **Set up a schedule:** For example, Australian students had a two-month break while Simpson's class was in school, but they chose to write the ebooks before they went on break rather than miss out on them.

- **Send reminders:** Simpson sent a reminder one week before books were due. She also included instructions for the next book when she sent out links to the books that had just been created.

- **Be prepared to make adjustments:** For example, Simpson and her partners felt that the books were spaced too closely together, so they adjusted the timeline and number of books. You might need to adjust the activity for students' ages and skill levels.

- **Help others troubleshoot:** No doubt, you will encounter problems with technology, especially when dealing with systems in other countries, so you must be patient while working through the glitches.

- **Encourage and engage participants:** Educators can stay connected between the books through email, Twitter, Skype, mail, and so on. Just keep the momentum going!

- **Encourage individuality:** Each classroom completes the books in a way that works for it, and no two are the same. Although students are collaborating, you do not have to work through the project in the same fashion as your collaborating classroom. You can instead make the project fit your individual curriculum.

Simpson's experience with creating her own project is mirrored by those of many educators around the world who share their stories on blogs and other social media. Sometimes it's better to jump in and create a project rather than wait for the perfect project to come along.

The Global Collaborative Project

Lesson planning for something that involves others can be either exciting or stressful, depending on the process. The following tips may come in handy in order to make this a smoother experience.

- **Find your passion and your purpose:** Finding the sweet spot of where to start allows you to become focused on the project's success and gives you more courage to push through any obstacles that may present themselves. For example, I have found that my students dive into deeper global collaboration a few months into the year after we have first created a sense of community in our own classroom.

- **Find your people:** If you are not connected to educators outside your school or district, now is a great time to become a *connected educator*, which in its truest form means to connect with others in a purposeful manner to better the way you teach. This can be done through connections you make both globally and locally.

- **Let go (a little):** There are bound to be things that do not go according to plan and projects that do not turn out the way you expected. That happens a lot in teaching. So allow a project to veer off the path if you can, and see where it goes. Often the best lessons come in unexpected ways.

Sometimes, educators are so inspired by a global project that they create their own. This is exactly what Kerri Thompson, a teacher from New Zealand, did after she participated in the Global Read Aloud. Here, she shares her story of how she used the idea of a preexisting project to create what has since become a multinational project:

> The concept of connecting learners through one book, after experiencing the Global Read Aloud, had me

thinking about our own authors in New Zealand and the possibility of initiating a collaborative project, which had a New Zealand focus. What an exciting prospect, connecting Kiwi kids through a book written by a New Zealand author with a New Zealand setting about New Zealand kids! And so the project was born— #NZreadaloud—One Book to Connect Kiwi Kids. (You may visit the blog at https://newzealandreadaloud .wordpress.com for more information about this journey.)

#NZreadaloud completed its third term [in 2016], having connected fifty-four teachers and approximately sixteen hundred learners this time around. The impact on learning has been exciting. Many teachers have emailed to inform me how much more enthused their reluctant readers are to engage in a book. (K. Thompson, personal communication, September 15, 2015)

Creating your own global collaborative project does not mean that your idea has to be unique; it means that you create a project that works for you. Find inspiration in what already exists, and then take the step toward creating something just for your students. By allowing yourself to be inspired, you will, in turn, be able to create unique learning opportunities that further student engagement in your literacy environment.

Ideas for Global Collaboration

Throughout the years, students have needed opportunities for global collaboration to enhance their engagement. Following is a list of ideas for quick and easy global collaborative projects. Most projects take only a small time commitment and just a few tools.

- Use Skype or Google Hangouts to show students how to do something, or pair up students as reading buddies. You can do the latter with students of different grade levels or even different countries or nationalities.

- Have students teach preservice or current educators how to use a blog or another tool that they have incorporated into their classroom.

- Have students create videos showcasing tips for how to complete a task or activity, like Mystery Skype, or something else that is uniquely theirs. Share the videos on YouTube or through Twitter to gain exposure.

- Create *Jeopardy!* trivia games about books, and play live against another class. This is a great way to share book recommendations and often takes only a small amount of preparation for the teachers involved.

- When working on fluency, record students performing picture book plays or silly poetry performances. Share these recordings with audiences around the world, and ask for their feedback using Google Forms in assessing students' speaking skills.

- Create nonfiction picture books or other writing for target audiences to read using Google Slides or Office Sway (https://sway.com). Have the audience read and assess using Google Forms to collect feedback.

- Have students create PSAs or other call-to-action videos and share them not only with your own school but also with the world through social media.

- Have students blog to share their self-selected work, or use blogs as a way to communicate with students and educators globally.

- Have students partner with another grade level or school as they edit and revise their writing.

- Create a hashtag to share what a day looks like for a student in your school. You might decide to share what the weather is that day, what your school looks like, or any other topic that is relevant to your instruction. Set a specific day to use the hashtag, and have students tune in to what is being shared.

While this is not an exhaustive list, it shows the myriad of options available to you as you begin to explore global collaboration. While it is important to ask others to consume what students create, it is equally important to receive what others produce. Engaging students in the give-and-take of the collaborative process allows them to become more connected to the world. Not only do they get to see their work's impact on others, but they also get to experience the impact themselves. Participating in global collaboration provides students with more immediate knowledge of the world that surrounds them as well as about what role they play in it.

Students do not develop just literacy skills through these types of projects; they also develop skills that help them be successful after their academic careers are over. By connecting students with others and providing opportunities to create for others, students can now see and hear the direct impact of their work and their voices. They intimately understand that they are only one piece of the very large puzzle that makes up our world. This is why global collaboration, along with providing students with an authentic audience (which will be discussed further in the next chapter), is essential to changing the way we teach, the way students learn, and how we connect.

Ten Tips for a Successful Global Collaborative Project

The following are ten tips for creating a successful global collaborative literacy project.

Be Simple

No collaborative idea ever took off if it required hours of explanation. Many global projects have grown large due to their simplicity, whether it is carrying a poem in your pocket for Poem in Your Pocket Day or sharing a read aloud for World Read Aloud Day. Having few guidelines to follow allows all participants to adapt a project to meet their needs; therefore, allowing for choice in how to participate is helpful. Figuring out the project's goal is helpful in allowing for more creative freedom. For example, assume the goal is for students to share book recommendations. Merely setting up a place to share, such as on an online bulletin board like Padlet (https://padlet.com), rather than establishing every single step, means that most students can participate (rather than just the few who can follow all the rules). Keeping the idea simple and straightforward allows it to be easily accessible for educators all over the world and for varying skill levels.

Make Sure the Idea Is Easily Translatable

This means it should be translatable in explanation as well as in participation. If your project focuses on a shared read aloud, then make sure the book is accessible outside your geographical location. The same goes for technology use. Schools are quite varied in their access to technology, so rather than selecting only a few tools for collaboration, leave it open for many types of tools, allowing for greater participation.

Don't Make Too Many Rules

If there are too many rules, the project may get stifled. Rather than planning a global project like a lesson, plan it with a beginning, middle, and end, but leave room for creative input along the way. A great collaborative project focuses on the product (for example, students share presentations on their cultures via a Skype call); however, how preparation for the project unfolds in the individual classroom may be quite varied depending on the guidelines and policies in place. Know what needs to be decided beforehand, and then allow other items to be developed during the project. This allows for more flexibility.

Invite Others to Contribute Ideas

Just because the project initially started as your idea doesn't mean it cannot get better. This is where the power of community comes in! Allow others to help shape the project, much like we allow students to help us in the classroom, and watch the project become even better. If the idea is to have your students teach other students how to do something, perhaps you can solicit input on what other students would like to learn. Or, if your students would like to write and share stories, they can survey students in other classrooms to find out what they want to read, which will lead to higher engagement. Realizing that others' contribution of ideas, particularly the ideas of those for whom the product is intended, will strengthen your project rather than undermine it is an important step toward better global collaboration.

Don't Get Stuck in a Rut

If you plan on continuing collaboration throughout the year or repeating it yearly, make sure to change it somehow. Otherwise, the project itself becomes just another thing to do instead of something to look forward to. Whenever you add a global component to your literacy instruction, vary it to some degree. Change your audience, your process, or even how students receive feedback so it stays fresh for both you and your students. Changes don't have to be major, just enough to keep the interest level high. While routine is a necessary component of our classrooms, global collaboration should not become an expected routine. Instead, you should use it as a way to increase student engagement and understanding.

Use Technology Tools for the Right Reason

In this age of technology, there is an impressive array of tools available for educators to facilitate global collaboration. Even with few resources, we can find many ways to facilitate connections to strengthen literacy instruction; what matters is determining what the tool should enhance and then finding a tool that can accomplish that goal. Global collaboration should not be tool driven but, instead, learning driven. That means that you should not create a project just for the sake of testing a tool; instead, create a project and then see what tools suit its purpose. If your goal is to have students communicate with others in order to develop their writing skills, then look at several different venues, and find the one that works best. Will a blog help you reach others? Will a chat facilitated in TodaysMeet (www.todaysmeet.com) meet your goal? Will letters sent through the mail promote learning? Whatever you decide to use should always benefit your instruction, not just test-run the tool.

Create a Community

If your project involves other educators, it is beneficial to find a tool that allows participants to create a community to share ideas. If it is manageable with email, use it; however, tools such as Facebook (www.facebook.com), Edmodo (www.edmodo.com), or Google Groups (https://groups.google.com) also come in handy when you want to communicate with a large group of people. These platforms provide a way for educators to share ideas and discuss the project without having to follow along in an email thread or speak via phone. Having a shared safe place to communicate is often what furthers teachers' quests for collaborative opportunities because it is within the community of other educators that they gain new ideas to pursue.

Be Accessible

As the head organizer, make sure you are easy to access and can answer questions as quickly as possible. Again, if you are the one initiating the project, make sure participants continue to have faith in you throughout the duration. That means checking email or whatever platform you are using for communication and responding in a timely manner. Many educators are nervous about collaborating with others since it involves spending precious time on something that is not completely within their control. Having easy access to the person in charge often calms the nerves and creates a more positive experience.

Trust Other People

Placing value on all the participants and their unique experiences only strengthens the project. Allowing others to share ideas and even implement ideas that may not have been a part of the original plan means that the process can develop into a more meaningful experience for everyone. In a project such as the NZReadAloud, one of the main components is the Facebook groups in which participants communicate and fine-tune the project. Some of the best ideas come from participants, not just the project creator.

Make It Fun!

Even if you are tackling serious subjects, include an element of fun. When teachers get excited, so do students. So whether it is the topic, the process, or how you connect, it's important to plan your project as a unique event to make the school day a better experience. Students should look forward to global collaboration, not dread it as another class requirement.

Global collaboration within our classrooms is not just an element that would be nice to add; it is something we must strive for as we plan the school year. Ron Schukar (1993) writes, "Children in this country must be provided an education that more than adequately prepares them for citizenship in the society and world they will soon inherit" (p. 57). We expect our students to graduate with skills they can apply in a global economy, and it is our job to prepare them well.

Do not be fooled into thinking that global collaboration is just about technology integration—far from it. Global collaboration is about letting students know that what they do matters to others and what they create can make a real difference in the world. Don't let a lack of technology stop you from becoming part of or creating your own global collaborative project. Turn that situation into a challenge to overcome, and work with the tools you have even if they are decidedly low-tech. Letters can connect your students to the world as well; what matters is that you get connected.

Reflection Questions

Before moving on to chapter 3, answer the following questions to reflect on this chapter.

1. What do you already do that lends itself naturally to adding a global component?

2. What kinds of preexisting projects might fit your needs?

3. Who could you potentially partner up with to create a global collaborative project?

4. How can you become a connected educator?

5. If you are already participating in global collaboration, what changes could you implement to make it even more meaningful to students?

Chapter 3
Global Connections With an Authentic Audience

"Who is this for?" one of my students asked. I had just finished explaining our latest project, which would last for the next several weeks—each student creating his or her own nonfiction picture book—and students were ironing out the final details before they began work. I smiled widely when I realized what my student really meant: Who is our audience? Who will see this besides you? Great questions, and ones that I was particularly pleased that my students were beginning to ask, because they had not started the year asking them. My students were becoming invested in the global literacy experience. By using technology tools to further their literacy identity, they were discovering a new world of opportunity to create.

Within our literacy instruction are amazing opportunities to have students' work travel beyond school walls. As discussed previously, we are no longer preparing students to become functioning adults just within our own local communities but within a global community.

Amanda Hager, an innovative learning coach in Elk Grove Village, Illinois, explains why she uses Twitter with her students, who are ages five to eleven. She writes:

> They should no longer be performing for us, but communicating and collaborating with the world. In doing so, learning takes on a new purpose, not to please my teacher, but because I matter and what I learn will help change the world. (A. Hager, personal communication, March 27, 2016)

What students create matters, and it needs to matter to a larger audience than just us. No longer should the teacher's voice be the only one that counts. Simply put, students' dreams of creation should not be confined within school walls. Providing students with an authentic audience becomes paramount in creating an exciting global experience and, ultimately, making our schools and world different.

Defining an Authentic Audience

The term *authentic audience* has been a favorite among educators for years, yet many may not be comfortable with what it means or where this supposed audience can be found. If you google the term, you will find many definitions, usually tied to the task of the audience, but the term actually encompasses much more. In my view, incorporating an authentic audience does not just mean blindly creating for others, but rather finding the right people for whom to create.

For example, my students choose a topic for their blogs so they can connect with like-minded students around the world. They share fan fiction, life hacks, sports news, or even just book reviews. Regardless of what they share, they want a great audience to create for and interact with. This is part of their blogs' purpose: to have a space where they can write whatever they like, which is often in juxtaposition to the more regimented or formal writing in which they are otherwise engaged. So, where is this audience my students are connected with? It turns out you can find it all around the world in other classrooms.

The first step to finding an authentic audience is for educators themselves to become connected in one way or another. Often we can find connections by joining social media platforms, such as Twitter, Facebook, Skype in the Classroom, or Edmodo, or we can connect with our local teacher communities. While there are many benefits to being a connected educator, one of the greatest is that we can more easily connect our students as well. If you are unsure of how to become a connected educator, you can begin by joining a preexisting global collaborative project (as discussed in chapter 2).

Having an authentic audience means that students are no longer creating a product just for the teacher or for themselves. For too long, students have come to school expecting to receive an assignment, followed the steps, and then turned in their finished products. Once the teacher assesses and returns the products with a grade, the journey of that assignment is done. Oftentimes, students do not even look at the feedback or internalize it in a way that helps them become more aware of their learning process and what they need to do to grow.

The very purpose of assessment is for students to receive feedback they can use to determine their own learning goals. We need to provide feedback that goes beyond what students do wrong or are missing on a particular assignment and instead provide information about what they need to work on as learners. That means feedback must be a continuous process that comes from multiple sources. This is why an authentic audience is important to the global literacy experience. Not only can we include sharing in the purpose of creating, but we also can let it help shape our entire creation process. It's not just that we are creating a product to share; we are creating the product for a targeted audience, thereby creating an avenue for receiving effective feedback that further shapes the learning process.

Asking Driving Questions

Providing our students with an authentic audience heightens student awareness of their own place in the world but, more importantly, develops a more joyful learning experience. Students become more invested and further engaged whenever a purpose for learning comes from outside their classroom. If you are contemplating bringing in an authentic audience for your students, there are a few driving questions that may help shape your quest.

What Is the Purpose of the Audience?

While students usually respond positively to creating for others, the audience must serve a larger purpose. Having an authentic audience can serve many purposes, such as giving students feedback, providing help with the creation process, or even teaching about other cultures throughout the collaborative process. Therefore, we must consider the audience's purpose before requesting an audience.

What Will Students Gain From the Experience?

While adding an audience is sure to change the creative process, it is important that students feel that they will inherently gain something from the audience experience. How will having outsiders as part of their learning benefit students? Deciding what you would like students ultimately to gain can help you as you seek out audiences with a specific plan in mind.

How Will You Safeguard Students During the Experience?

Depending on your students' age group, parents or administrators may be wary of bringing a virtually unknown entity into the classroom community. You may even have some initial concerns. It is important to consider how to handle student privacy requests and how to share and protect student work. Many educators choose to have students share using only their initials, their first name, or even an assumed pen name. Other topics of concern depend on the types of tools being used to share work. You should discuss these topics with students, no matter their age. We should engage even our youngest students in conversations about shaping their own digital footprint whenever it fits the learning. Setting up guidelines for students to follow every time they collaborate helps them automatically think about how they function online.

What Are the Technology and Connection Needs?

While computers and other connection devices are becoming more commonplace in schools in North America, access to technology can still greatly differ based on the economic makeup of one's school. It is important to consider what types of tools, technological or not, we use to engage an audience. Will students have access to devices individually, or will they need to share? Do we need other tools to record and then share videos? How will the audience access the products we create, and how will we facilitate communication? Knowing one's own limitations, as well as possibilities, is important when considering what type of authentic audience experience we can provide.

Finding an Authentic Audience

There are a few key considerations to keep in mind as we create opportunities for an authentic audience. Some may seem like basic common sense but are still important to mention here. Before we share student work with a wider audience, we must make sure we do the following.

Obtain Parents' Permission to Share Student Work

While many districts have technology permission forms that cover the privacy question, it is vital that parents and guardians have a say in how their children's work is shared with the world. We should also offer parents the opportunity to see the products themselves. If a student's parents do not agree with the purpose, then create an alternative for that student.

Obtain Students' Permission to Share Their Work

We tend to think that all students want their work to be public, yet that is not always the case. We should give more thought to student privacy as far as *what* they would like to share, not just *how* they share it, so having a conversation with each student about this is important.

As the year progresses, many educators choose to have students delve into more personal topics, and those products often do not lend themselves to sharing with a large audience. Considering whether students want to share something is important to protecting the trusting relationships you build within the classroom. This consideration also should apply to individual students. While some may be ready to share everything with anyone, others may be more hesitant. It is not our job to judge but instead to support their journey and help them become more comfortable with sharing, and also to teach them what is appropriate to share and when. This is a good opportunity to discuss some of the dangers of interacting with others online and some of the safeguards students can take to be secure in an online environment.

Gather the Tools for Success

If you work in a school with limited technology, or even in a school that has no technology, then you must consider these limitations. That does not mean, however, that you cannot find an audience. Perhaps you can find an audience in your local community; perhaps your class can write letters to share via mail or the newspaper. Once again, as you begin your journey, it is important to remember that a global literacy environment does not hinge on the use of technology, but rather on the use of connections. Often it is our own creativity (and sometimes even district or school policies) that limits us more than the actual tools we have or don't have.

Get Administration on Board

While it is not always necessary to get administrative approval, since policies seem to differ from school to school, it is common courtesy to at least let administrators know of your plans. The administration is often excited about new and exciting school projects and might love to see them develop and unfold rather than find out later. A project might become a guiding light for others who want to try something similar, which then helps administrators guide collaboration, if needed. Administrators want to know who their global experts are so these experts can help them when other educators want to embark on a similar endeavor.

Creating Projects for an Authentic Audience

With these common-sense guidelines in mind, we can further our exploration into creating projects for an authentic audience. Depending on the project, the following process may help you consider what your own process should be.

Establish Your Purpose

When considering an authentic audience, knowing the project's purpose is vital to its success. Planning from the end goal rather than the beginning may be helpful since you can decide what you would like students to get from the audience. Know what standards or objectives must be covered. Questions to guide your planning process include: Can this project involve multiple learning objectives? What will students need to accomplish to show mastery of these objectives? How will the audience be involved? Should they only be involved at the final stage after the creation is completed, or should they be involved during the creation process? Too often, we wait to ask for feedback until the end of a project, yet a student's creative process can be greatly improved if the student receives feedback *during* the process. The project determines when it is appropriate for others to become involved, so knowing your purpose helps you decide that.

Collaborate With Students

Involving students in planning the project is a good way to increase student buy-in and sustained engagement. Students can offer unique insight into the process, including how it could be more meaningful to them. The questions they ask can help you finalize details before the project goes live. Do not skip this step—it can help foster deep, long-lasting effects on the student experience. It's also important to discuss the standards or objectives that you will explore through the project, as it allows for further student agency. When students know how they are supposed to develop their knowledge, they can set out on a more certain path.

Research Your Audience

Do some initial research on the people who have volunteered to be your audience. Doing a Google search or even a Skype call to find out who is on the receiving end strengthens the connection for students as they see whom they are sharing with. Connecting with the people who will experience your product means that students gain a clearer understanding of how their products might be viewed.

Start the Project

At some point, the preparation is over and the project must begin. Keep the audience as part of the creation process either by discussing what they are expecting with your students or by checking in with them from time to time. While the intent is not to make the final assessment the project's focus, it is important for students to remember that the project will travel past their classroom walls. Take as much time as needed, since it is important that students do not feel like they are always rushing from one project to the next but, instead, can enjoy the project they are currently working on.

Connect Throughout the Project

How often you check in with your audience depends on the type of project you are creating. It is a good idea to keep some communication open if you need to ask your audience questions. Having open communication can help remind students that this is not just for your eyes. Even if the communication is just teacher to teacher, students can learn a lot from asking questions.

Share the Final Product

Once students are ready to share, the audience is finally fully involved. With the advent of Google Classroom (https://classroom .google.com), Microsoft OneNote (www.onenote.com), and other cloud-based creation tools, sharing has become remarkably easy. Experiment with how you want to share before you reach that point in the project. This way, you can make sure that your audience can actually access the product when needed.

Receive Feedback From Your Audience

While your audience can give feedback in a multitude of ways, knowing what is most useful to students should guide how you would like to incorporate the feedback process. The following are just a few examples of how you could receive feedback.

- Receive feedback live. If students are using Skype to share the project, then the audience can give feedback through Skype, and students can immediately process it.

- Receive feedback via preset Google Forms that you email to the audience ahead of time; be sure to include guiding questions.

- Receive feedback from your audience within the product itself using a tool such as Google Docs (www .google.com/docs).

Whichever way you communicate, make sure that it is as simple as possible for the audience to access. Communicate with your audience about what type of feedback you want to help them keep the purpose in mind. Keep the number of questions to four or fewer so as not to overburden your audience. If you are in doubt, ask your students what they would like to know, and then try to incorporate their ideas into your feedback request.

Have Students Self-Assess Based on Audience Feedback

Once you present the feedback to students, give them an opportunity to reflect on it and set further learning goals based on the audience's reaction. This does not have to follow a formal learning plan but can be a quick reflection that students keep in a reader's notebook or e-portfolio. It can even be a spoken reflection with a partner. What matters is letting students digest the feedback and then apply it to their learning. This is the most important part of the journey with an authentic audience.

Now that their product has been assessed by someone else, they need to assess it as well. Once students reflect, they also should have the chance to self-assess their project using the same assessment format that you use. Allowing students the chance to see their project through the teacher's eyes gives them more ownership over the creation process and helps further their learning journey.

Give Students Your Final Assessment

After students reflect and assess, they should somehow pass on the knowledge they gained to you, the teacher. You may have them share their assessment via a short reflection or rubric, depending on the chosen format. It is then up to you to determine the final assessment alongside the student. If the assessments do not align, you can use a verbal conference to further discuss each student's strengths and goals. We often spend the least amount of time on the process's final step—handing assessments back to students—yet it is this step that deserves more time and attention. This step allows students to understand what they must change in order to improve their learning as well as their process and how it may affect a global audience.

When the habit of adding on an authentic audience is in place, the need for it becomes even more apparent. We should incorporate an audience not simply because we live in a world where connecting with others is easy but because it offers students a way to discover how much they can affect others and vice versa. If we truly are creating a global literacy classroom that functions on students knowing their own literacy identity, students must also know where that identity fits into the world. For example, how will their work as writers shape others? How will the knowledge they gain as readers shape their own personal journey?

Not only should we search for authentic audiences for our students, we should *become* authentic audiences as well. This ensures that our students are exposed to other learning communities and helps them further reflect on themselves as learners and individuals.

Reflection Questions

Before moving on to chapter 4, answer the following questions to reflect on this chapter.

1. Where is there a natural opportunity in your curriculum for students to create for others?

2. How could an authentic audience enhance what students are already doing?

3. What are some ways your students can become connected with others?

4. How are you connected to other educators?

5. What tools do you need to create a global literacy experience?

Chapter 4
Students as Creators, Not Just Consumers

Whenever I start a new year with students, I am reminded of all that I do not know. Last year's students are so familiar, but they have passed on to the next grade level. As each new year begins, I am faced with more than one hundred twenty new students with one hundred twenty new needs, dreams, and journeys to undertake. Yet, within that first week of our literacy experience together, we start to uncover and develop our reading and writing identities. We search for favorite books to share, and we write about ourselves as authors. We start to have conversations that weave the thread of the community we create.

We lay the foundation for students to see themselves as members of an ever-expanding society in which their own identities as creators will be immersed. Those first few weeks with so many new students are never without challenges, and yet, being part of a journey in which students become re-energized as they see how their work and their voices can matter to more than their immediate peers is a driving force for many. It is for these students that we pursue a global literacy environment.

Why We Create

A driving force for many educators, myself included, as our class-rooms have evolved, has been changing the student identity from that of learner only to *creator*. Students tell us that they do not want to be fed information for simple test regurgitation; nor do they feel like they are creating much when we ask them to make a poster or PowerPoint presentation for classroom consumption. Instead, they want knowledge that they can work with to create something uniquely theirs. Our job as teachers is to provide them with not only the tools to do so but also the opportunity. Students should not be waiting for the *real world* to do real work. They are already living in the real world; the real world is in your classroom as well!

While there are still times when students can learn something as a foundation for later learning, mostly our literacy classrooms should involve a "make something" process. No longer should we expect stu-dents to be school writers but, instead, *real* writers. No longer should students expect merely to read books but, instead, to become book critics and connoisseurs while discovering their literacy identity in a classroom filled with student choice and voice. This process involves adding tools to our classrooms that allow students to embrace their maker-creator identity. Yet, it is not just about the tools. Tools provide us with the instrument for inviting students to create content that others view. What really matters is what students want to create—the product—and the effect that product might have on the world.

For too long, students have hidden their maker-creator identities from us in school, rather than allowing these unique traits to shape their learning journeys. How many times have we experienced stu-dents not sharing the writing they do *outside* of school because they don't see how it connects with what they do *in* school? Sometimes students don't share what they are most passionate about because they don't see how it relates to anything in school.

One way to tap into students' passion is to incorporate the Genius Hour concept or Innovation Day into the school experience. Denise Krebs, a second-grade teacher in Bahrain and coauthor of *The*

Genius Hour Guidebook: Fostering Passion, Wonder, and Inquiry in the Classroom (Krebs & Zvi, 2016), says this about Genius Hour:

> Genius Hour is a regular block of time, one or more hours in a week, when teachers give students autonomy to choose what they want to learn. Students are guided to develop an inquiry question based on something they are curious or passionate about. Then the teacher gets out of the way and lets students learn purposefully. Students are entrusted to wonder, learn, create, research, take action, produce, inquire, and master.
>
> Genius Hour students become fearless learners, who share their genius with the world by making their creations, projects, and learning visible. (personal communication, March 25, 2016)

Incorporating Genius Hour is a way for students to create, explore, and think critically within the learning community, and you can adapt it to fit many literacy experiences. You can offer free choice to help students become more creative thinkers, or you can set it up under a chosen unit of study to help students reflect on, symbolize, or elaborate on a text they just finished reading. It is up to us to tap into students' creativity and offer opportunities within our global literacy classroom for students to showcase all their talents, not just those they think fit within a certain topic or project. As you start to plan for more meaningful creation opportunities for your students, it may help to reflect on the following big-idea questions.

Will the Creative Process Be Meaningful to Students?

As discussed previously, without a purpose that involves an authentic audience, students may see little need for engagement beyond the get-it-done mentality that is so common in school. Within our literacy instruction, we should consider what students can create with the knowledge they are gaining. What real purposes, as opposed to contrived ones, can we offer them, and how can we encourage them to personalize the process to be more meaningful? Will having students create give them a reason to become more engaged, or will they meet the idea with disdain?

Will the Creative Process Be Authentic?

While the practice of students as creators is nothing new (after all, most teachers can remember creating projects for school), there has been a significant change in focus on the purpose behind the creation process. It is important that students see the creative process as a natural extension of what they are already doing rather than as an add-on. This harkens back to the days of book report projects, in which students would be asked to write a report after reading a book and then create something to go along with it, such as a diorama or poster. While this is certainly an attempt to have students create, it does guarantee further learning since there is no choice behind the process. Ensuring that what students are creating makes sense in the context of what they are doing is vital for student buy-in.

Is There an Audience for the Final Product?

Not everything students do lends itself to an audience. When students choose to create for an audience, we should be sure that their creation is suited for as well as interesting to that audience. Asking for people outside your classroom to invest their time in reviewing student work means that it needs to be worth their time as well. If in doubt, ask a colleague to evaluate the project with you.

How Will the Project Support Students' Learning Journeys?

Everything we do in our classrooms must benefit our students. So while global collaboration can certainly be used as a way to try out new ideas, those ideas should lead to a more meaningful experience for students, not just a way to cover content more efficiently. Will students gain knowledge that they could not obtain in another, simpler way? If the answer is no, then perhaps the creative process is not worth the time investment. Are the physical products really worth our time? If not, how can we change that?

Student creation can feel like a beast to be tamed—messy, noisy, and directionless. However, we can set up parameters within our learning communities to navigate the creation process in a meaningful way without it becoming chaotic. Just because students are creating rather than consuming does not mean you are not needed. The teacher's role is to teach when needed, guide when needed, support when needed, redirect when needed, and step away when needed.

We must know our students well, even in the upper grades, to best support them in their creative endeavors. Yet, what matters more than knowing our students is giving students the opportunity to know themselves—their own strengths and weaknesses—and to set meaningful goals for how they want to develop as learners and as individuals. We can do this beautifully within our literacy environments because sharing the reading and writing process naturally develops relationships. Through writing and sharing, students might find connections and commonalities with peers they never knew existed before.

When students write, many will gravitate toward a natural peer-to-peer writing process within the classroom. Involving an outside peer or creativity mentor adds to the critical lens through which the students view their work and provides them with an opportunity to further reflect. When someone outside the classroom offers suggestions, my students often listen. If we want to further extend those relationships, we can look outside our classroom to the larger community.

We also must realize that the creative process can look vastly different from one student to the next. Some students want to create with their hands, others want to use technology, and still others do not want to create but rather get from point A to point B in the fastest way possible. We must offer classroom experiences in which there is room for all these types of learners and where the literacy identity students develop is allowed to change, depending on the task at hand.

What matters is that we support students as they explore, challenge them, and provide many opportunities to do so in a meaningful way. We want school to matter, not just to be something students have to do. Everything we do within the literacy classroom should build toward something larger than us—to develop more thoughtful human beings, not just faster readers or better writers.

Every moment that we teach, we make a decision of whether we want students to listen to us share information, or if we want students to work with information that we discover together. It is a choice we make and not one that we should take lightly. While there is space for students to gain foundational knowledge in a lecture format, this should not be the most commonly used approach for students to learn. Instead, you should use lectures sparingly and purposefully as a way to create shared knowledge and also model your own thinking. If you need a lecture to create the foundation of further exploration, then let students know that they will receive information they need to build on, and then get to the point.

Too often we share stories, add too many details, and speak too long, thus taking time away from student exploration. Simply put: sometimes we, as teachers, can be the barriers to deeper student learning experiences, but it does not have to be that way. We can create literacy environments in which all students feel that they have a voice, that they have a choice in how they learn, and that their work matters to the teacher as well as to the outside world.

Simple Literacy Project Ideas

Creation within the literacy classroom can start with the very books we read and the writing we already do; however, our creations must have a meaningful purpose and focus on choice. For instance, not all students want to make a 3-D model, and we need to accept that. Following are a few ideas for the different products students can create in the literacy environment.

- Stop-motion movies to display information they learned

- Brief persuasive speeches about a sculpture, highlighting why it is the best sculpture ever made (even if it's not)

- Informative websites based on research students have done in any content area

- Shared Padlet bulletin boards (to gather information as your students connect with other classrooms and learn about different cultures)

- Interpretive sculptures based on a well-loved book's theme

- Fan fiction published on a site such as Wattpad (www .wattpad.com)

- Book trailers using Animoto for Education (https:// animoto.com/business/education)

- Plays and short skits persuading others to read a book

- Editorial letters to be published in the local newspaper

- Persuasive letters to the school board and administration to change school policy

- Sculptural models of a solution to a problem that students research

- Poetry or picture book performances to practice fluency

This is only a short list of what students can create and is meant to inspire ways in which you can make student creation a natural enhancement of what you already do. Many of these ideas came from my own students through the years as they asked to create more meaningful work. These ideas have all been tried and tested by students ages nine to thirteen years old. The common thread for many of these projects is that they had a real purpose stemming from student ideas, rather than being forced on students as a way to show learning. Instead, the process and the final product are meant to inspire action in others, even if that action is as simple as urging them to read a certain book.

To encourage more ideas, ask your students what would help them become more engaged. What would help them feel more connected with the world as they develop their literacy identity? After all, they are the ones who are learning; they are the ones we are trying to inspire.

When writing this book, I knew I had a choice to make—list all the tools we can use to create with students or simply share the need for creation. I chose the latter, knowing that we all are faced with varied access to tools as well as different motivations and ideas. Yet, inviting students to be creators is a natural extension of everything discussed in this book.

Students who thrive in their literacy environments have more energy to do something meaningful with their learning, whatever that something may be. When we offer students opportunities to create in our classrooms, we provide a natural outlet for exploration of the outside world. Students no longer have to wait until after school to be writers, YouTubers, or whatever other alternate identities they might have. When we choose to create a global literacy environment, we can foster and strengthen those identities with what we do in our classrooms.

Reflection Questions

Before moving on to the conclusion, answer the following questions to reflect on this chapter.

1. How can you uncover students' "secret" identities as creators?

2. How can students become creativity mentors for each other?

3. How can you add meaning through creation to the projects you already do?

4. How can you use the creation process to strengthen your literacy classroom?

5. How can you develop or showcase your creative process?

Conclusion

Many incredible teachers dedicate their lives to the future of our world by choosing to teach. However, there also are many educators and, indeed, entire school systems focused on the "just fine" method of teaching—as long as students progress, then we are doing just fine. Just fine teaching does not lead to greatness; it does not lead to schools where students are excited to be stakeholders. It does not lead to a change in the negative perception in the media and in political discussions of schools that surround us. Just fine teaching will lead to just fine students who may not change the world. Perhaps this is a simplistic idea, but it holds true.

Many of us entered education to create a better place for those who follow in our footsteps, and being a just fine educator will not fulfill that purpose. Yet the path to change is often filled with self-doubt and excuses. We are often our own worst enemies when it comes to change, leaving us assuming that we cannot be like schools or educators we admire. We may assume that being great is something bestowed on others because of certain special talents or circumstances. But that is not always true. Becoming great often starts with making a small change that leads to another small change. Soon, all those small changes add up to a large change. Becoming great is a journey we decide to begin and then complete, constantly reassessing and reevaluating along the way.

In our literacy classrooms, we are afforded a luxury and curriculum that not many other teachers get. Within the reading, writing, speaking, and listening that we do are ample opportunities to really get to know our students in a meaningful way; what we do lends itself naturally to exploration of self as well as ownership over what kind of people we are.

Within our classrooms, we must therefore create opportunities in which students can engage in a meaningful way that supports their natural development as global citizens. When students can see that their work has a direct impact on the world around them, their desire will grow to be a part of the solutions we need to make this world better. When we ask our students to become critical readers, to create meaning with their words, infusing our literacy communities with global collaboration is a natural fit.

We communicate in this world in so many ways, and we must make sure to practice this within our lessons. That may seem like a given, yet how many times have we witnessed teaching, or even taught in a way, that was not authentic or even meaningful to students? How many times have we been complicit in creating artificial experiences in which students saw little value or relevance? We do not have to teach this way. Within the very content we cover is what makes us essentially human: communication of emotions, ideas, and thoughts. This is what we must tap into as we strive to make schools different, where both student and staff are not just going through the motions so the student can move on to the next grade.

One barrier we might face by becoming more connected is increased workload. Our literacy instruction already needs to incorporate reading, writing, speaking, and listening skills, meaning we already have a full plate. I know teaching English to seventh graders within a forty-five-minute period each day is never enough, and the inherent absurdity of the forty-five minutes means that every minute truly counts. Therefore, it is only natural to assume that adding any activity described in this book will just be more work. However, it does not have to be this way if we focus on one great idea at a time. There is no need to try to do everything at once; there is no deadline when all ideas must be implemented to have value.

What matters is sorting through the change we need most urgently and then focusing our energy on that idea. If we try too many things at once, we simply create more risk of burning out and giving up. We should focus only on what we can actually implement. We are under siege with decisions, initiatives, and political talk that do nothing to ease our workload. While we can't ignore these challenges, we must be sure our voice is louder than the critics' negative voices; we can choose not to spend as much energy on those doubts.

Instead, we must save our energy for ideas that are within our control, those changes we can make within our own literacy environment. We can focus on our successes rather than our failures. When we believe that what we do can become even better, imagine the learning students can experience!

The literacy classroom of the future will not be run by robots, nor will it require all students to sit behind a computer screen waiting for the next lesson so they can check it off, one step closer to graduation. It is a classroom where our knowledge of books is not just limited to those we read ourselves, where writing is not just for the teacher, and where authentic global collaboration is a pillar of learning. It is one where we are continually changing with the world outside our classroom, where students' digital footprints are already being shaped, and where teachers feel supported by a larger community outside their own.

The beauty of this vision is that it is not something we have to wait for, nor something we need more funding to attain; we simply need to take the first step toward change. The future waits in our global literacy classrooms. We can make it happen right now.

References and Resources

Allington, R. (2002). *The six Ts of effective elementary literacy instruction.* Accessed at www.readingrockets.org/article/six-ts -effective-elementary-literacy-instruction on April 10, 2016.

American Academy of Child and Adolescent Psychiatry. (2011). *Teen brain: Behavior, problem solving, and decision making.* Accessed at www.aacap.org/AACAP/Families_and_Youth/Facts_for_Families /FFF-Guide/The-Teen-Brain-Behavior-Problem-Solving-and -Decision-Making-095.aspx on March 22, 2016.

Anderson, R. C., Hiebert, E. H., Scott, J. A., & Wilkinson, I. A. G. (1985). *Becoming a nation of readers: The report of the Commission on Reading.* Washington, DC: National Academy of Education.

Azzam, A. M. (2007). Special report: Why students drop out. *Educational Leadership, 64*(7), 91–93. Accessed at www.ascd.org /publications/educational-leadership/apr07/vol64/num07/Why -Students-Drop-Out.aspx on January 3, 2015.

Boston Latin School. (n.d.). *BLS history.* Accessed at www.bls.org/apps /pages/index.jsp?uREC_ID=206116&type=d on April 2, 2016.

Busteed, B. (2013, January 7). *The school cliff: Student engagement drops with each school year* [Blog post]. Accessed at www.gallup .com/opinion/gallup/170525/school-cliff-student-engagement -drops-school-year.aspx on October 10, 2014.

Friedman, T. L. (2005). *The world is flat: A brief history of the twenty-first century.* New York: Farrar, Straus and Giroux.

Harper, D. (2003). Students as change agents: The Generation Y model. In M. S. Khine & D. Fisher (Eds.), *Technology-rich learning environments: A future perspective* (pp. 307–330). Singapore: World Scientific.

Krebs, D., & Zvi, G. (2016). *The Genius Hour guidebook: Fostering passion, wonder, and inquiry in the classroom.* New York: Routledge.

Lenhart, A. (2015). *Teens, social media & technology overview 2015.* Washington, DC: Pew Research Center. Accessed at www .pewinternet.org/2015/04/09/teens-social-media-technology -2015/?utm_content=buffer0d98d on May 18, 2016.

McLeod, S. (2014, December 22). We need schools to be different. *Huffington Post.* Accessed at www.huffingtonpost.com/scott-mcleod /we-need-schools-to-be-dif_b_6353198.html on June 28, 2016.

Mendizabal, E. (2010). *On the origin of think tanks: Newspapers.* Accessed at https://onthinktanks.org/articles/on-the-origin-of -think-tanks-newspapers on March 2, 2016.

Ripp, P. (2013). Where in the world are they? Students find out with Mystery Skype. *Learning and Leading With Technology, 40*(5), 30–31. Accessed at www.learningandleading-digital.com/learning _leading/201302/?pg=32#pg32 on June 30, 2016.

Ripp, P. (2015, June 23). *The future of literacy* [Blog post]. Accessed at https://pernillesripp.com/2015/06/23/the-future-of-literacy on March 17, 2016.

Schukar, R. (1993). Controversy in global education lessons for teacher educators. *Theory Into Practice, 32*(1), 52–57.

Snelling, J. (2016). Empowering student voice. *Entrsekt, 2*(4), 24–30.

Soundout. (2015, April 3). *Definitions of student voice.* Accessed at https://soundout.org/definitions-of-student-voice-2 on May 1, 2016.

Surowiecki, J. (2004). *The wisdom of crowds: Why the many are smarter than the few and how collective wisdom shapes business, economies, societies, and nations.* New York: Doubleday.

United States Postal Service. (n.d.). *Postal history.* Accessed at https:// about.usps.com/who-we-are/postal-history/welcome.htm on March 23, 2016.

Wadsworth, R. M. (2008). Using read alouds in today's classrooms. *Leadership Compass, 5*(3), 1–3.

Solutions for Creating the Learning Spaces Students Deserve

Solutions Series: Solutions for Creating the Learning Spaces Students Deserve reimagines the norms defining K–12 education. In a short, reader-friendly format, these books challenge traditional thinking about schooling and encourage readers to question their beliefs about what real teaching and learning look like in action.

Creating a Culture of Feedback
William M. Ferriter and Paul J. Cancellieri
BKF731

Embracing a Culture of Joy
Dean Shareski
BKF730

Making Learning Flow
John Spencer
BKF733

Reimagining Literacy Through Global Collaboration
Pernille Ripp
BKF732

Wait! Your professional development journey doesn't have to end with the last pages of this book.

We realize improving student learning doesn't happen overnight. And your school or district shouldn't be left to puzzle out all the details of this process alone.

No matter where you are on the journey, we're committed to helping you get to the next stage.

Take advantage of everything from **custom workshops** to **keynote presentations** and **interactive web and video conferencing**. We can even help you develop an action plan tailored to fit your specific needs.

Let's get the conversation started.

Call 888.763.9045 today.

SolutionTree.com